IMAGES
of America

HARRISBURG
STATE HOSPITAL
PENNSYLVANIA'S FIRST
PUBLIC ASYLUM

On April 14, 1845, Act 288 passed the Pennsylvania legislature and was signed into law. The act was "To establish an asylum for the insane poor of this commonwealth, to be called The Pennsylvania State Lunatic Hospital and Union Asylum for the Insane." (Courtesy of the Pennsylvania State Archives.)

ON THE COVER: Patients gathered on the lawn in front of the male ward nine and ten annex. Though no description is available for this undated image, one can assume that these patients were probably having a picnic based upon their attire and the fact that some of them are eating watermelon. (Author's collection.)

IMAGES
of America

HARRISBURG
STATE HOSPITAL
PENNSYLVANIA'S FIRST
PUBLIC ASYLUM

Phillip N. Thomas

ARCADIA
PUBLISHING

Published by Arcadia Publishing
Charleston, South Carolina

Library of Congress Control Number: 2012946148

For all general information, please contact Arcadia Publishing:
Telephone 843-853-2070
Fax 843-853-0044
E-mail sales@arcadiapublishing.com
For customer service and orders:
Toll-Free 1-888-313-2665

Visit us on the Internet at www.arcadiapublishing.com

*This book is dedicated to all the former patients
and staff of Harrisburg State Hospital.*

CONTENTS

ACKNOWLEDGMENTS

The author would like to thank William R., John P., and the Pennsylvania State Archives for their help in making this book possible. Unless otherwise noted, all images appear courtesy of the Pennsylvania State Archives; Record Group 23, Records of the Department of Public Welfare; Office of Mental Health; Harrisburg State Hospital, Series 23.146, 23.188, 23.194.

This book is the result of research conducted at the Pennsylvania State Archives and does not represent the opinions or views of the Pennsylvania Department of Public Welfare, OMHSAS, or the Harrisburg State Hospital. The author does not have a clinical background and has never worked at the Harrisburg State Hospital.

Faces of patients have been blurred in some photographs in order to protect their privacy.

INTRODUCTION

During the 18th century, a new approach to the treatment and care of the mentally ill was starting to surface that would come to be known as moral treatment. Prior to this movement, the mentally ill were often stereotyped as animals. The very few hospitals that existed during this period were not so much treating the mentally ill; rather, they were simply warehousing them out of site of the public. Moral treatment, simply put, was a movement to treat the mentally ill less as an uncontrollable animal and more as a person with an illness. One of the key moral treatment figures in the United States was Benjamin Rush. In 1812, he wrote *Medical Inquiries and Observations upon the Diseases of the Mind*, the first textbook published on the subject in the United States. Rush limited his practice at the Pennsylvania Hospital in Philadelphia to only those with mental illnesses. The Pennsylvania Hospital, which was a private institution established in 1751, did not have proper facilities to care for mentally ill patients, so Rush led a campaign in 1792 to construct a new ward solely for these patients.

In 1832, the managers at the Pennsylvania Hospital decided a new facility was needed to alleviate the crowded conditions of its wards, in which mentally ill patients now outnumbered those with physical illnesses. In 1835, a 101-acre farm was purchased in West Philadelphia, and the cornerstone for the Pennsylvania Hospital for the Insane was laid on July 26, 1836. Dr. Thomas Story Kirkbride was named superintendent of the new facility, which opened on January 1, 1841. Dr. Kirkbride played an important role in the early treatment and care for those with mental illnesses, publishing a book in 1854 entitled *On the Construction, Organization, and General Arrangements of Hospitals for the Insane*. The majority of new institutions for the mentally ill built over the next 45 years would be based upon his book. Several other private hospitals had also opened in the United States in the early 19th century with the sole purpose of caring for those with mental illnesses. The Frankford Asylum for the Insane was established in Philadelphia in 1813, and in 1821, the Bloomingdale Asylum opened in New York. None of these early hospitals, however, were public institutions; only those who could afford to pay for treatment were admitted. As the number of people living in large cities began to rise during the Industrial Revolution, so too did the number of mentally ill. Because the cities lacked proper facilities to care for the indigent insane, most were either living in jails or on the streets.

Dorothea Dix was an essential figure in establishing better living conditions for the indigent insane. Originally a school teacher, she traveled the country inspecting the mostly appalling conditions of the jails and poor houses in which the mentally ill lived. For each state she visited, she would prepare a "memorial" bearing her findings. The memorial would be delivered to the state legislature by a friendly and well-known political figure. Many of her memorials resulted in the establishment of new state-run hospitals. In 1845, Dix presented a memorial to Pennsylvania lawmakers that resulted in the founding of the Pennsylvania State Lunatic Hospital and Union Asylum for the Insane. Patients from all parts of the state would be accepted at the new institution, at the expense of the counties from which they came.

In the spring of 1845, the Pennsylvania legislature appointed a group of five men to a commission. These men were given the responsibility of establishing and constructing the first public asylum for the insane in Pennsylvania. They were instructed to select and purchase a tract of land no less than 100 acres, situated within 10 miles of the city of Harrisburg, at a cost of no more than $10,000. Initially they were interested in a farm known as the Ridgway Farm just north of the city, but the purchase fell through. So in November, the commissioners purchased the Sales Farm, a 130-acre tract about a mile north of the city. Once the land for the new hospital was secured, the commissioners then traveled to Philadelphia to visit the Pennsylvania Hospital for the Insane. They were given an extended tour of the hospital and grounds by Dr. Kirkbride; there they gained "much valuable information with regard to the plan, arrangement, and internal economy of a well constructed building." Upon their return to Harrisburg, the commissioners adopted a resolution that the hospital would be of "Kirkbride-design."

Progress on the hospital was put on hold for several years until deficiencies in the original legislation could be corrected. On April 25, 1848, the building commissioners met again. Three additional men were added to the group, and the words "Union Asylum" were dropped from the name. On May 10, the group appointed architect Samuel Holman of Harrisburg to design and oversee construction of the hospital. However, two months later, the commissioners dropped Holman as the architect and instead adopted the plan and specifications furnished by John Haviland. Haviland's proposal estimated that construction of the hospital would cost $100,000. The switch in architects appeared to have been based on Haviland's reputation and experience rather than any dissatisfaction with Samuel Holman. Holman would later build some of the outbuildings, including the wash house and the carriage house. John Haviland opened his practice in Philadelphia in 1816 and had several major structures in the city to his credit, including Eastern State Penitentiary and the Franklin Institute.

According to the 1845 legislature, the new hospital was to be "plain and substantial, with all modern improvements, to accommodate 250 patients." In July 1848, the commissioners went out to the farm and agreed upon the location of the building, marking its corners with stakes. On April 7 of the following year, the cornerstone was laid by Gov. William F. Johnston. Haviland estimated that the building would be completed by November 1850, but when the commissioners paid him the final installment of $55,800 in December 1850, it became obvious that the hospital was not going to be completed on time. On the afternoon of February 14, 1851, a group of nine men met at Coverly's Hotel in Harrisburg. These men were appointed by the governor to be hospital trustees; they would be responsible for running the institution. At their first meeting, they elected Dr. John Curwen of the Pennsylvania Hospital in Philadelphia to be the superintendent. Haviland turned over the completed building on June 19, 1851.

One

PENNSYLVANIA'S FIRST PUBLIC ASYLUM

During the spring and summer of 1851, the hospital was furnished and made ready to receive its first patients. Much of the furnishings, such as bedding, clothing, utensils, and furniture, came from Philadelphia. On October 1, 1851, the new Pennsylvania State Lunatic Hospital was declared open. Five days later, the first patient arrived, Elizabeth B. of Londonderry Township. The 42-year-old woman was suffering from dyspepsia and melancholy, most likely brought on by the loss of two of her three sons to scarlet fever the previous July. By late October 1851, there were a mere 12 patients at the hospital, six males and six females. At the end of the first year, the population had increased to 37, with 24 males and 13 females. The original price for room and board was set at $2 a week. The sale of produce from the farm also brought money into the hospital. Even after her successful lobbying efforts to establish the hospital, Dorothea Dix continued to show great interest in the institution and its patents. She raised money in Philadelphia to provide the hospital with a bowling alley, two buildings for reading rooms and museums, several horses, a carriage, magic lanterns with slides, musical instruments, and many books. In consideration of the great services Dix rendered, in 1853, the board of trustees authorized the superintendent to receive and treat without charge any one person recommended for admission by Dix. The patient recommended by her entered the hospital on March 6, 1853, and remained until death in 1895. By the end of 1853, the population of the hospital had increased to 182 patients. During the Civil War, the hospital provided assistance to the soldiers at Camp Curtin. Those who were too sick to be cared for at the camp were brought to the hospital for treatment. Thousands of pounds of beef and ham, as well as gallons of coffee, were served to the soldiers. Clothing was prepared for the sick, and soldiers were allowed to use the hospital's bathrooms and laundry facility.

The Main Building consisted of a center administration section with a set of wings extending in a linear direction on either side. The wing to the right of the administration section was designated for female patients and the left for male patients. The wings, which housed the patient wards, were arranged so that the second set of wards receded 20 feet behind the first, and the third the same distance. This arrangement was to ensure that the most fresh air and sunlight possible was allowed into the building. The set of wards immediately adjoined to the administration section were three stories tall, with the ground floor containing accommodations for staff and nurses and the second and third floors for patients. The second set of wards were also three stories tall and contained patient rooms on all three floors. An infirmary was located on the fourth floor junction between the first and second wards. A third set of wards were completed in 1852; they were two stories tall with accommodations for 300 additional patients.

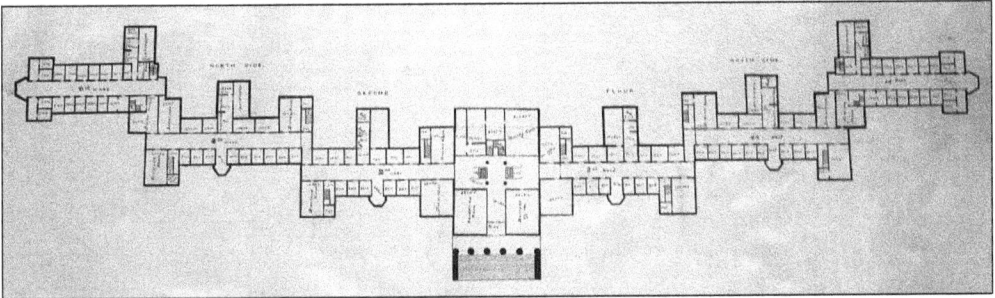

This is a photograph of the actual blueprints for the main floor, which currently reside at the Pennsylvania State Archives. The total length of the building was 680 feet.

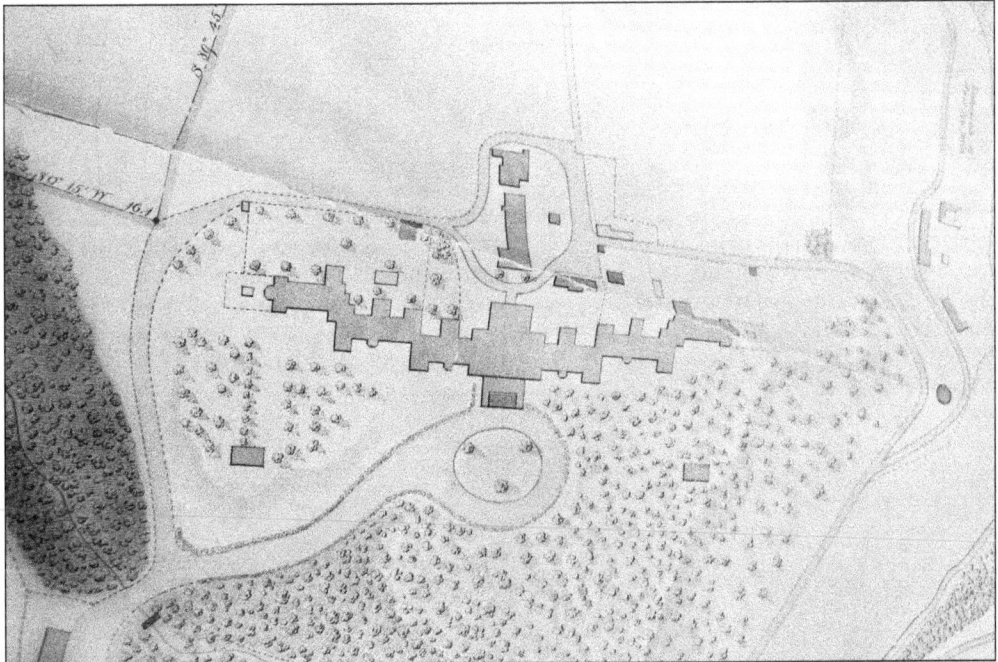

This ground map of the hospital dates to around 1875. The largest structure on the map is the Main Building, with the driveway in front of it and two small cottage buildings on either side. Eighty feet behind the Main Building is the bakery and the laundry. Located in the cellar of this building were the boilers for heating the hospital and a room for storing up to 150 tons of coal. The structure to the far rear is the Fan House.

Early problems with the new building were described in a letter from superintendent John Curwen to Dr. Kirkbride in November 1851, just one month after the hospital officially opened. Some of the problems described in the letter were poorly fitted windows with gaps large enough to fit one's finger through and doors that would not properly latch due to the settling of the building. Gusts of wind from the previously mentioned windows would blow open the doors of patient rooms. These problems were all corrected the following year.

INSANE ASYLUM
HARRISBURG

The administration section was four stories tall with a large Tuscan portico, topped off with a dome from which one could see for miles in any direction. On the ground floor were apartments for the steward and matron, as well as a kitchen. On the second were offices and reception rooms for visitors, and the third contained an apartment for the superintendent and his family. On the fourth floor was a chapel and six more bedrooms. This undated stereoview card is currently the only known image of the original administration section. (Author's collection.)

This undated photograph shows a female ward around 1880. The wards were pretty much identical, consisting of a long corridor with rooms on either side. This construction method was known as a double-loaded corridor and was common among Kirkbride-design buildings. Each ward had its own dining room, dormitory, parlor, bathroom, water closet, and several single-patient rooms.

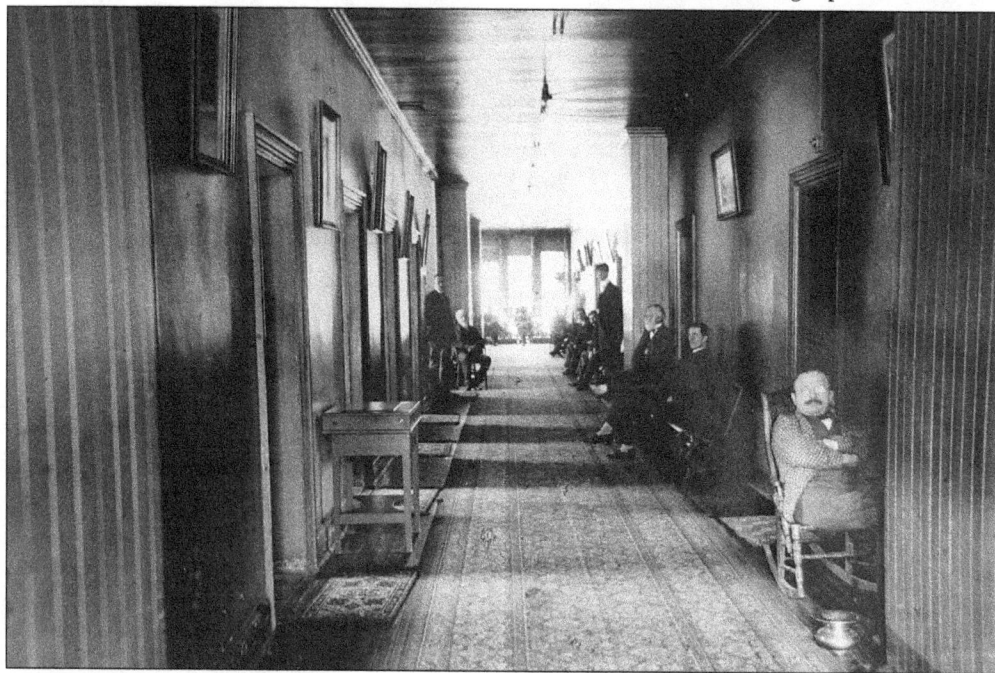

The wards were unusually dark and cramped in comparison to other hospitals of this design. The hallways were only 10 feet wide; once filled with chairs and other furniture, there was little space left. This photograph of a male ward was likely taken around 1900. Patients would often congregate in the small hallways during the daytime.

The Main Building had constant problems with poor heating and ventilation, both of which were seen as critical instruments in the treatment of the insane. A fan house, seen on the right in this image, was constructed in 1867. Steam-powered fans forced fresh air into the building via a series of tunnels dug in the dirt cellar. The building on the left is the bakery.

Ventilation flues can be seen lining the walls of a female ward in this photograph. The flues were added to the building in conjunction with the new fan house in an effort to deliver fresh air throughout all the floors. Steam radiators located in the cellar would warm the air during winter months. Additional steam radiators were also added in the parlors, where the flues were not big enough to adequately warm the rooms.

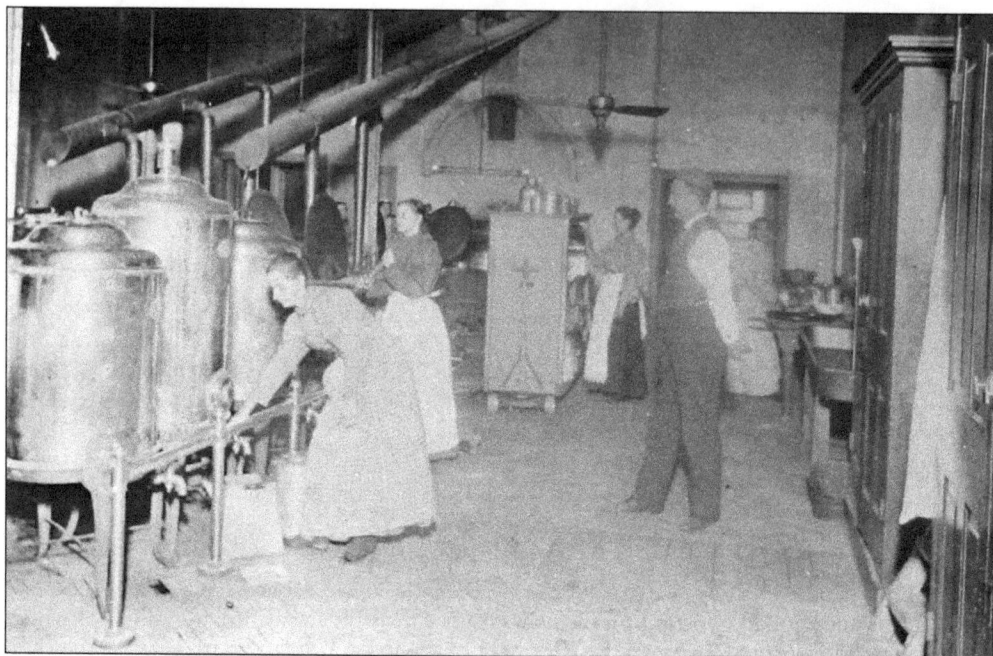

A kitchen was established in a separate structure near the bakery. Food was transported by cart to the Main Building, where a series of dumbwaiters were used to elevate the food up to the dining rooms in each ward. A woman can be seen in this undated photograph preparing one of the food carts.

Ward dining rooms were small and cramped, as evident in this undated image. Patients would eat meals "family style" with attendants sitting at the head of the table. Patients were required to remain at the table until all were finished eating.

John Curwen served as the first superintendent until March 1881, when the hospital trustees failed to reelect him. Though never brought up on any official charges, Curwen became frequently absent from the hospital in the 1870s and was even accused of mishandling hospital funds. After leaving Harrisburg, he went on to accept a similar position at the newly finished Warren State Hospital in northwestern Pennsylvania. Curwen also served as a building commissioner at the state hospitals in Dixmont and Danville. He retired in 1900 and returned to Harrisburg to live with his daughter. He unexpectedly died on July 2, 1901. Jerome Gerhard was elected as the second superintendent.

Pool tables could be found throughout the hospital and were enjoyed by staff and patients alike. Pool remained a very popular form of recreation even throughout the final years of the hospital. Other early forms of recreation included reading, carriage rides, polyorama cards, and magic lantern shows. Much of the early recreation items were donated by the Philadelphia Fund, organized by Dorothea Dix.

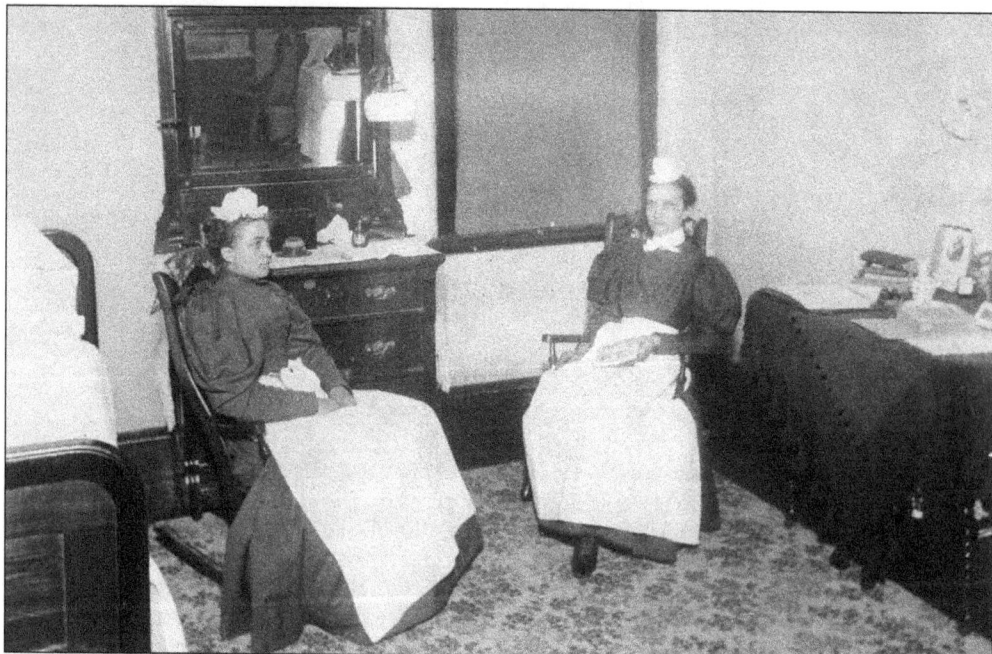

Two women sit in a staff living quarters around 1900. The staff lived in rooms on the ground floor of the building.

Women pose for a photograph in the sewing room around 1900. Able female patients were often tasked with creating or mending patient garments. They also worked in the laundry.

The caption on this photograph reads, "Miss Kinter sits at her desk in the marking room around 1900." Notice the decorative iron bars outside the windows, installed to keep patients from falling or jumping out of the windows.

This undated photograph shows three men in one of the male wards. Each ward had an iron staircase at either end that allowed for a fast and safe exit in the event of a fire.

Female attendants pose for a picture around 1900. The rear of the Main Building is visible in the background.

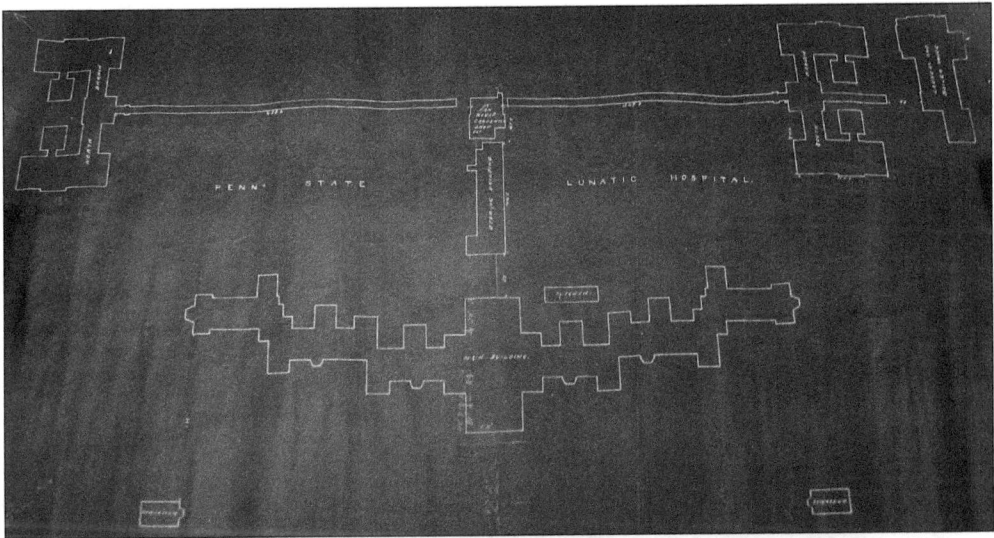

By 1885, the hospital was becoming overcrowded. With the wards of the Main Building well over recommended capacity, it was realized that expansion was going to be necessary. Plans for two new buildings were drawn up and appropriations were made for their construction. As seen on this ground map, the new buildings, known as North and South Branch, were built behind the Main Building. They would accommodate 152 additional patients each.

Construction of the Branch Buildings began in 1886 and finished in 1888. Both buildings were put up rather hastily in order to quickly alleviate overcrowding in the Main Building. Plans were made to add porches and center towers to both buildings after they were occupied, but these plans never came to fruition. The North Branch Building, seen in this photograph, was used for male patients.

Female Wards 9 · 10   *P. S. L. H.*

The South Branch Building, seen here, was used for female patients. Both buildings were constructed primarily of wood, which was not the preferred material to use in hospital construction due to the always-existent threat of fire.

Male Wards 9 · 10   *P. S. L. H.*

This unreleased postcard shows the North Branch Building as it appeared during the reconstruction of the hospital. To the left, a small portion of the Male Recreation Building is visible. (Author's collection.)

Seen on the right in this image is a long covered corridor that connected the South Branch Building with the rest of the hospital. An identical corridor connected the North Branch Building on the other side of the Fan House. Both corridors were torn down in 1908 when the Main Building was replaced.

This undated image shows the view inside one of the covered corridors. Patients and staff would use these corridors to move between the buildings during inclement weather. They were also used to transport food from the kitchen to the ward dining rooms.

This photograph shows a day room in the North Branch Building, also known as Male 9 and 10, around 1910. The first floor in both Branch Buildings contained two large day rooms as well as some single and double bedrooms. These large rooms would later be used for gatherings such as religious services and holiday activities.

The second floor of both buildings contained large open dormitories. Four rows of beds were lined up side by side. This method made for maximum patient capacity during a period when overcrowding problems plagued the hospital. But it was done so at the expense of patient privacy. The second floor also contained a few single bedrooms.

Two

ADMINISTRATION

Only 30 years after construction finished, the Main Building was in poor shape. It had been constructed hastily and with poor materials, and conditions were so deteriorated by 1881 that architect John Sunderland was hired to inspect the building. Sunderland found it "impractical to alter or make it in any way safe except by the expenditure of a large sum of money. You would only have an old building very expensive to keep in repair." In 1884 another architect, this time Addison Hutton, wrote an ominous report on the poor state of the building. Yet the state legislature refused to grant funds for anything but minor repairs and alterations to the existing structure. So desperate were the hospital trustees and superintendent to have the building replaced that over the next 10 years the only money spent on the Main Building was what was imperative to keep it in operation. When Henry Orth became superintendent in 1891, he dedicated four pages of his first annual report to what he referred to as the "deplorable and almost uninhabitable condition of the building." Finally in May 1893, the state legislature passed an act that appropriated $100,000 for the replacement of the administration section of the Main Building. In November of the same year, ground was broken for the new building. It was to be of the best design possible, built of fireproof material, and without expensive ornamentation or decoration. By 1894, the new Administration Building was well on its way to completion. Despite the fact that the legislature only granted appropriations for a single new structure, Superintendent Orth and architect Hutton went ahead in drawing up plans for a new set of patient buildings. The two men designed the plan for new buildings following an emerging trend in hospital construction known as the "Cottage Plan." The idea was to have individual buildings for each type of illness as well as for male and female patients. Twelve new buildings were designed, including patient wards, homes for the staff, a chapel, and a kitchen.

The new Administration Building was opened on May 2, 1895. Eight days later, staff had finished moving out of the Main Building. As part of the 1893 act that appropriated money for the new Administration Building, it was now mandatory to demolish the administration section of the Main Building; demolition would take only 26 working days to complete. With the loss of the administration section also came the loss of the hospital chapel, which had been located on the fourth floor. The exterior of the new Administration Building was built of red brick; the walls were 20 inches thick with a hollow space in the middle to prevent dampness. The interior was made up of iron beams supporting wooden floors, doors, and trimmings. Stairways were made of iron so as to be fireproof in the event of an emergency. The building was purposely designed in a modest Colonial style to set it apart from the strong classical styling of the Main Building.

· PLAN ·
OF
· ADMINISTRATION BVILDING ·

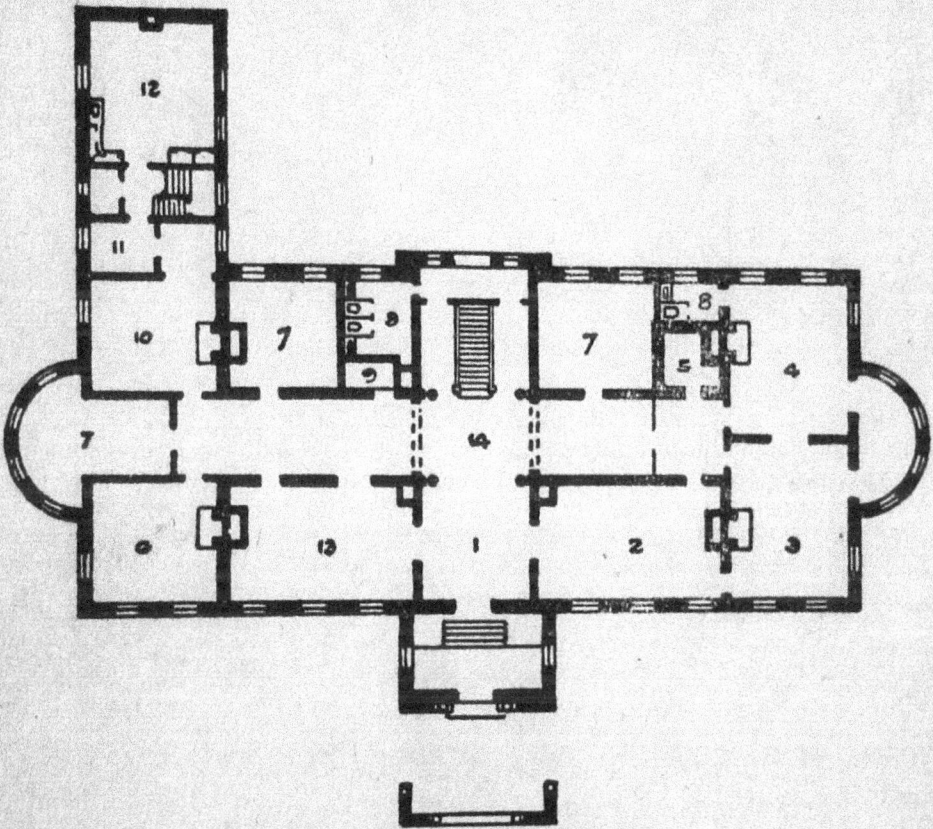

· FIRST FLOOR PLAN ·

· INDEX ·

1	MAIN ENTRANCE	8	TOILET
2	STEWARDS ROOM.	9	ELEVATOR
3	SVPTS PRIVATE OFFICE.	10	DINING ROOM
4	TRVSTEES ROOM	11	PANTRY
5	VAVLT	12	KITCHEN
6	LIBRARY	13	WAITING ROOM.
7	OFFICE.	14	CORRIDOR.

This floor plan for the new Administration Building shows the layout of the first floor, which was used mostly for offices. The second floor contained apartments for the medical staff, and the third floor was the residence for the medical superintendent and his family.

The main entrance on the first floor opened up to a large lobby with a tile floor. This floor also contained executive offices, a reception room for patients, a library, an officer's dining room, a kitchen, and a vault.

Taken in the front office on the first floor, the caption on this 1895 photograph reads, "Mr. Livingston at right; Dr. Wright at left." (Courtesy of William R.)

Three women pose for a picture in the officer's kitchen. This kitchen prepared food for the administrative staff; additional kitchens were also located on the second and third floors.

The gentleman in this photograph is Superintendent Henry L. Orth. Opposite Orth is his secretary. The picture was taken around 1900.

The assistant superintendent sits with other staff in his office around 1900.

This 1900 photograph shows an unknown room; based solely on the decor, it might have been the superintendent's office. The portrait above the fireplace is of Dorothea Dix, who was instrumental in helping to establish the hospital. The portrait was donated to the hospital by the trustees of the Philadelphia Fund after her death in 1859. It still hangs in a room on the third floor as of 2012.

This 1905 photograph shows the well-manicured lawn and fountain that greeted all new patients arriving at the hospital. Much of the work done on the grounds was completed by patients under the supervision of attendants.

This unreleased postcard shows the view every patient would have seen as he or she approached the hospital up the driveway. From this angle, the Administration Building actually looks larger than it really is due to the L shape of the building. One might speculate that architect Addison Hutton knowingly designed the building this way so it would appear larger to those arriving at the hospital.

The rear of the Administration Building is seen in this photograph from around 1930. The tunnel and walkway were later removed, probably when the new Admissions Building was constructed in 1951.

This 1885 photograph of the hospital band was presumably taken in the now demolished chapel, which was located on the fourth floor of the old administration section. It would be many years before a new chapel would be constructed. During this time, the large day rooms in the Branch Buildings were used for religious services and for large gatherings such as at Christmas.

This aerial image of the Main Building shows the gap between the two wings where the administration section once stood. Much work had to be done to demolish such a critical section of the building. Steam had to be rerouted, and a new water tank had to be installed in the laundry tower since the hospital's fresh water tank had been located in the dome.

This photograph, taken around 1899, shows the female wing of the Main Building with part of the new Administration Building in front. Patients would continue to live in the wings for several years until appropriations were granted for additional new structures. As new patient buildings were completed and opened, the wings were systematically abandoned and torn down.

Overcrowding problems continued through the end of the 19th century, with as many as 10 patients living in rooms designed for four. There was also a very concerning lack of competent employees due to a combination of better paying jobs on the docks of Harrisburg and the poor employee living conditions at the hospital. In previous years, lesser pay was made up for by room and board on the grounds, but this benefit was far less enticing with the crowded living conditions that both patients and staff had to endure. Patient beds can be seen lining a ward hallway in this undated photograph.

Three

CONSTRUCTING A
COTTAGE PLAN HOSPITAL

From 1893 to 1898, the annual reports of the trustees and superintendent repeatedly called for the continued rebuilding of the hospital. But each year, the state legislature failed to appropriate any money for new buildings. A paragraph from the 1894 report of the superintendent reads, "For years the buildings of this institution have been condemned as unsatisfactory, as not adapted for their purposes, as unhealthy on account of the saturated condition of the walls, and of course not desirable for the care of our inmates." Despite the new Branch Buildings, which were constructed only a few years earlier, the problem of overcrowding continued to worsen, so much so that new admissions had to be restricted to only those with the most recent diagnosis or those with the most severe cases. By 1898, there were 907 patients in a hospital designed for only 700. With the dormitories of the Branch Buildings filled to capacity, beds were now being placed in hallways to accommodate the growing number of patients. Nurses were forced to sleep in rooms on their wards; some slept in rooms with as many as four to five other nurses. In what seemed like a desperate act, in 1898, the hospital trustees asked the state for immediate funds of $120,000 for a new chapel, kitchen, and two staff homes, presumably to be constructed in the gap where the recently demolished administration section once stood, but appropriations for these requests were not granted.

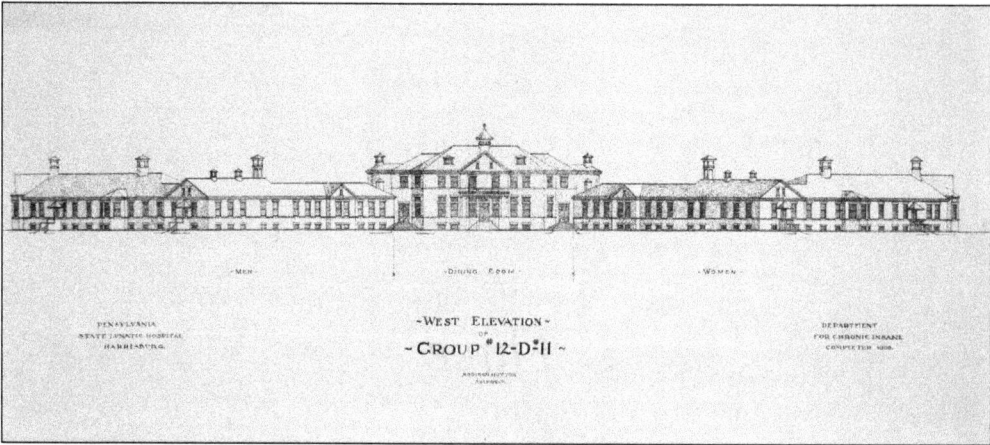

West Elevation of Group 12-D-11

Finally in 1899, much to the relief of hospital staff, the state legislature granted appropriations for a new patient building. The new building was designated as Male 1 and 2 and Female 1 and 2 for the Helpless and Harmless but was also known as the Infirmary. Though it was referred to as two separate buildings in annual reports, it was essentially one large building.

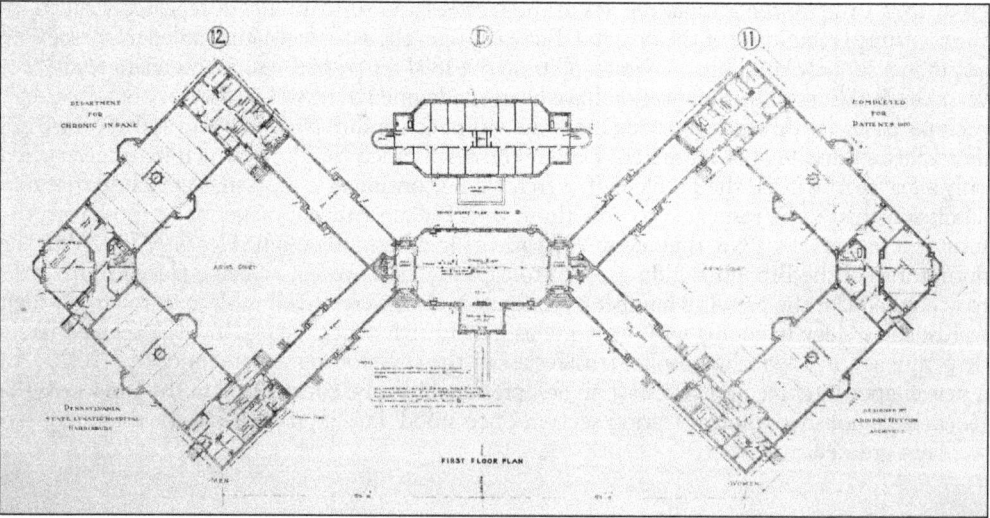

First Floor Plan

Designed by Addison Hutton, the building was one of his more unique designs. It was comprised of large open dormitories and day rooms, with male patients residing in the left part of the building and female patients in the right. The two sides were joined in the center by a two-story section that contained a few bedrooms and a common dining room. Ground was broken in April 1899 with a projected completion date of May 1900.

The Infirmary was finally completed well behind schedule on January 18, 1901. In the annual report for the year 1900, Superintendent Orth commented that the building was "large, airy, well-heated and ventilated, and constructed with some novel features." It was designed for use by patients who were mainly bedridden and required special food and nursing. Five days after the building was completed, 225 patients were transferred out of the old wards of the Main Building and into the new structure. On February 26, demolition commenced on the vacated old wards. Bricks were preserved for future use, while iron beams and stone from the foundation were used to build a tunnel and walkway to the new patient building.

This photograph shows the female day room in the new Infirmary around 1902.

This undated photograph shows several women in the Infirmary dining room. The caption reads, "Helps dining hall, 75 chairs, photo date unknown."

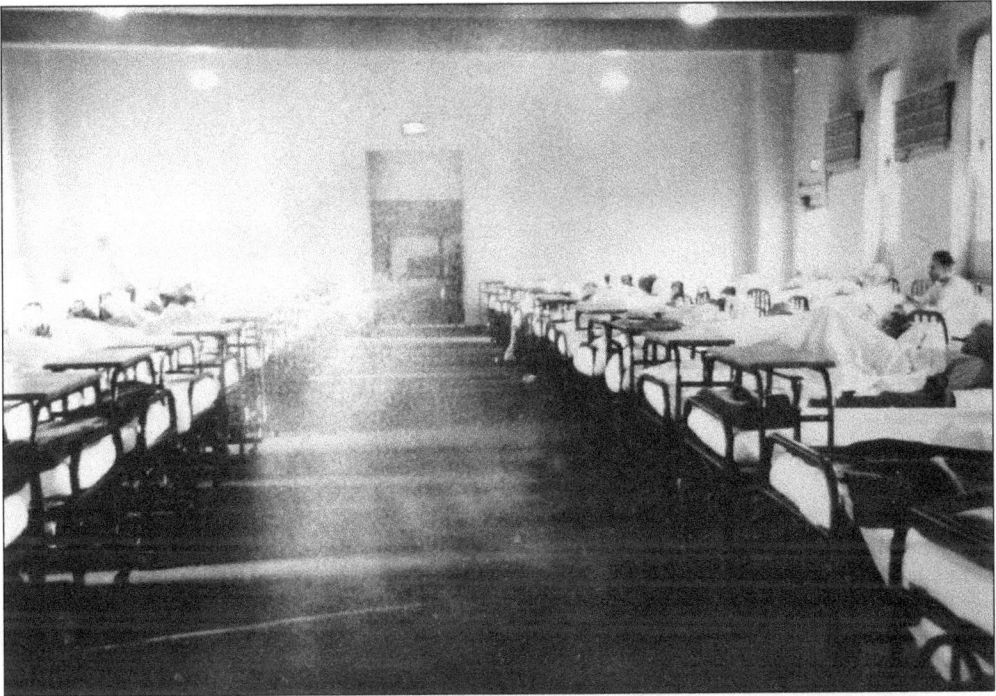

The two images on this page give a good comparison of how the wards changed throughout the years. The photograph above was taken in 1945 in the Male 1 ward of the Infirmary.

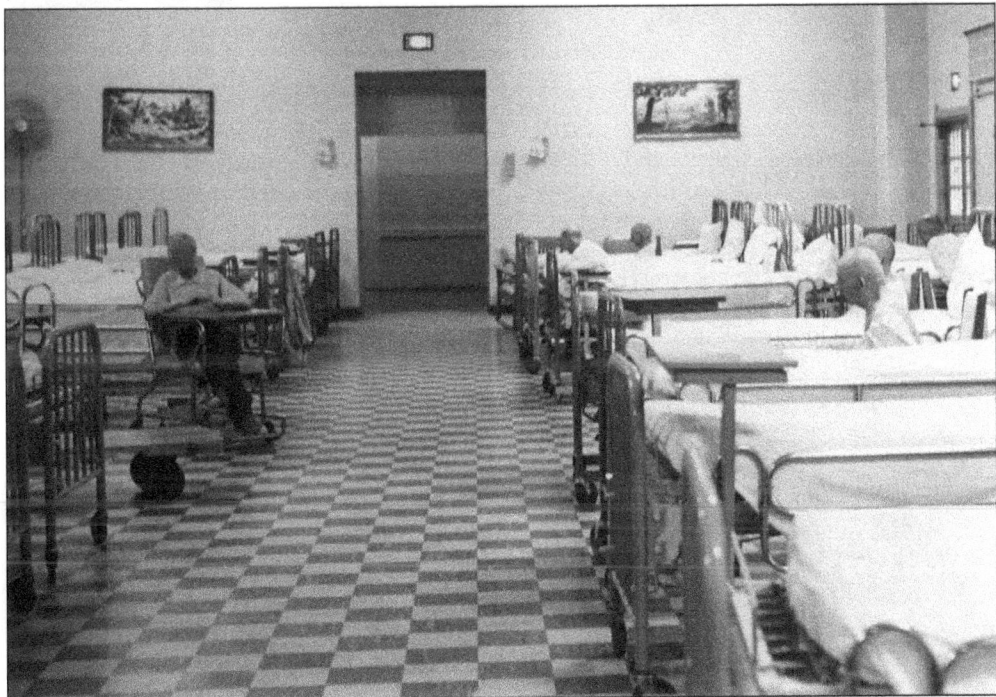

This photograph was taken in the same ward, at almost the exact same angle as the image above, except 25 years later in 1970. The Infirmary would be used almost exclusively for geriatric patients until its closure.

During a late session of legislation in 1901, appropriations of $253,000 were made for the construction of four additional buildings, with work planned to commence in the spring of 1902. Plans were for a new kitchen, morgue, male acute ward, and male violent ward. However, Gov. William Alexis Stone made drastic cuts to the appropriations before the trustees could award any contracts, and the total allotted for the construction was reduced to only $130,000. Several alterations were made to the planned buildings as well as reductions to their overall size to try to build them with the money in hand. But after much deliberation, the trustees surrendered their attempts to build all the planned buildings and instead moved forward with only the kitchen (seen in this photograph) and the morgue.

· KITCHEN BVILDING ·

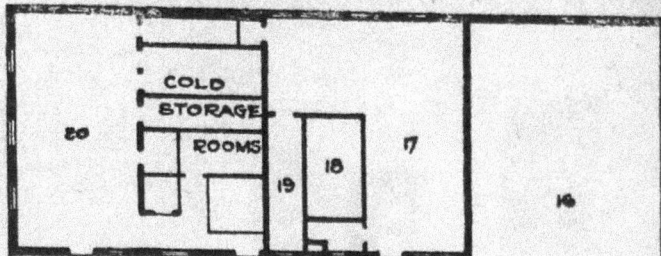

COLD STORAGE ROOMS

· INDEX ·

1 MATRONS STORE ROOM.
2 MATRONS OFFICE.
3 STEWARDS DINING ROOM
4 STEWARDS OFFICE
5 PANTRY
6 HALL
7 CLOAK ROOM
8 DINING ROOM.
9 DISH PANTRY
10 INCLINE TO SVBWAY
11 POTS AND PANS.
12 SCVLLERY
13 KITCHEN
14 COAL
15 TOILETS,
16 STORE ROOM
17 BAKERY.
18 OVEN.
19 BREAD ROOM
20 BVTCHER SHOP.

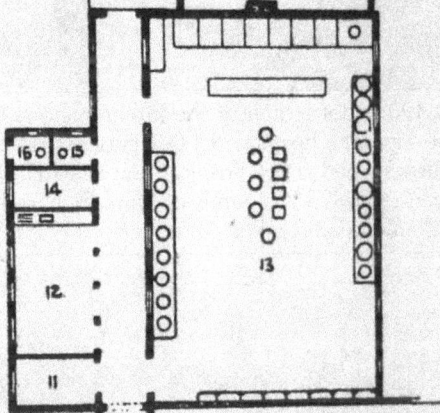

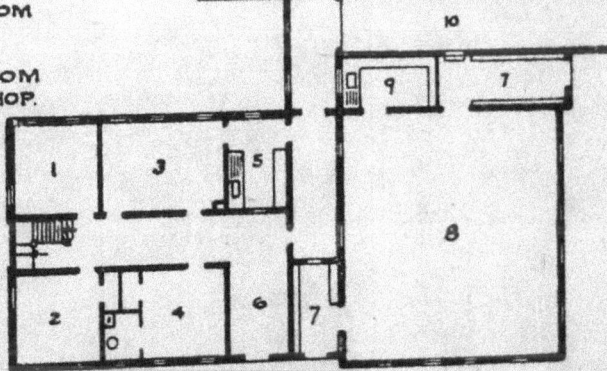

· FIRST FLOOR PLAN ·

The new kitchen was redesigned and its size was reduced in order to build it with the allotted appropriations. Construction finished on September 17, 1903. The new kitchen featured a dining area for patients, a butcher shop, a cold storage room, and a bakery. For those unable to use the new dining room, a series of tunnels connected it with the rest of the complex so that food could be transported by cart to the ward dining rooms in each of the patient buildings.

This early 1903 photograph of the kitchen shows a relatively modest setup. The kitchen was designed to support a hospital of 1,000 patients. The 1904 annual report listed the large amount of food that was used at the hospital that year: 173,793 pounds of beef, 29,109 pounds of butter, 12,162 dozen eggs, 17,159 pounds of ham, 51 barrels of salt fish, 9,025 pounds of coffee, 1,699 barrels of flour, and 205 gallons of oysters.

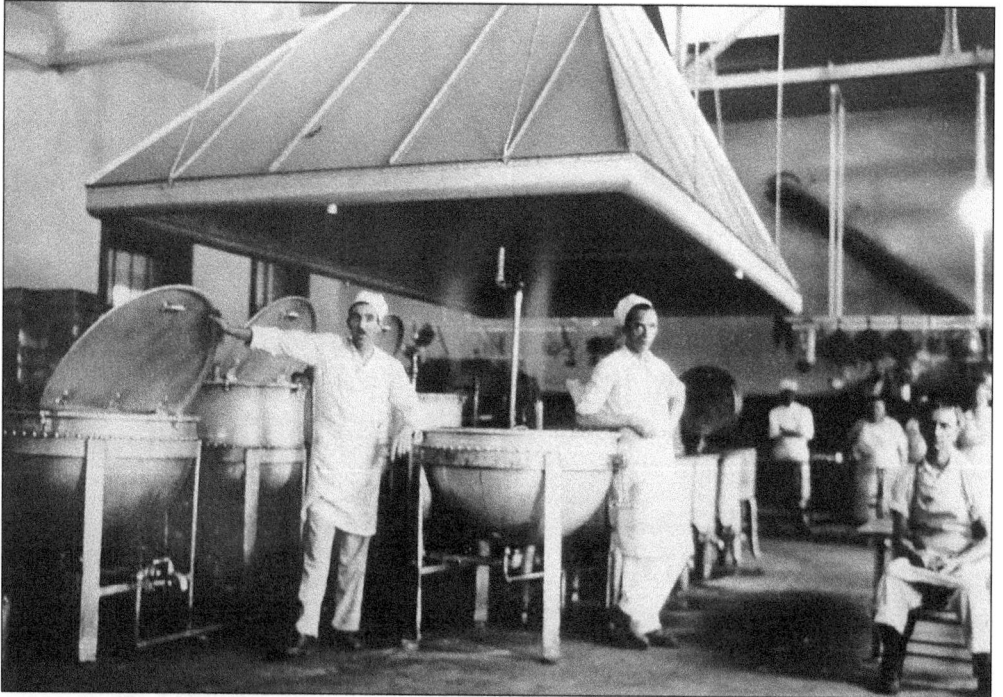

This 1930s photograph shows a much more crowded kitchen. As the number of patients at the hospital exceeded 1,500, the small kitchen struggled to feed the ever-growing population. The lack of a proper preparation area also made things more difficult, as workers had to do all their prep work, such as peeling potatoes, in the already cramped and hot kitchen.

The Cold Storage Building contained electric refrigerators constructed of wood. The refrigerators could hold up to 20 beef carcasses and contained a "furnished box" for storage of milk, butter, vegetables, and fruits. With the completion of the Cold Storage Building in 1904, the practice of harvesting ice during the winter from the hospital pond and storing it in the Ice House was abandoned.

This photograph is of the hospital bake shop around 1920. Along with potatoes, bread was a staple at the hospital. Wheat, flour, and other ingredients were all grown on the hospital farm, which made it very inexpensive to produce.

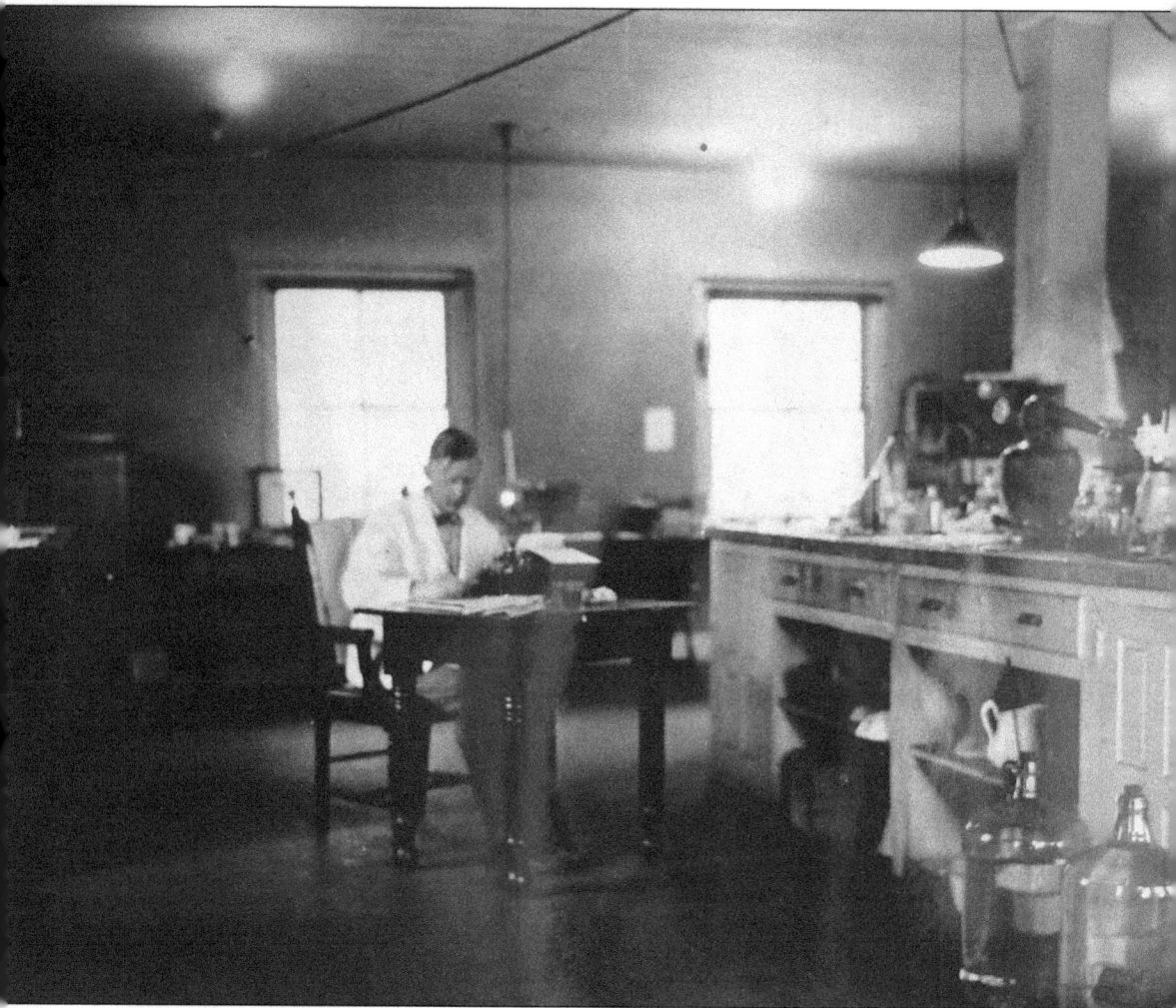

The new morgue building was completed in 1903. It was built in a valley to the south of the main hospital complex and just west of the waterworks. The building was two stories tall; the first contained an examination area and coolers, and the second held a pathology laboratory. A few years later, a tunnel was completed that connected the morgue to the Female Convalescent Building. The placement of the morgue in the valley near the waterworks was no accident. During the early 20th century, one of the biggest responsibilities of the pathologist was to conduct regular tests on the hospital water supply and to make sure the sewage disposal plant was functioning properly. Great efforts were made in the early years to outfit the laboratory with the best possible equipment.

The pathology lab, seen here around 1950, was viewed as crucial in researching the cause of mental illness. When allowed by a patient's family, post-mortem examinations were conducted. During the early years of the hospital, much attention was given to examining the deceased patient's brain. The pathology lab would also conduct a urine analysis on each new patient admitted to the hospital.

Despite being set on fire by a patient and repeated break-in attempts, as of 2012, the pathology lab still appears much as it did in these photographs.

Appropriations of $132,500 were approved for new male patient buildings at the end of 1903. Construction commenced in 1904 on the Male Psychopathic Building, Male Convalescent Building, and the Male Dangerous and Destructive Building. The legislation required that they be of fireproof material and free of unnecessary and expensive ornamentation. Two temporary structures were also constructed in 1904 to alleviate some of the overcrowding. These temporary wards were not asked for by the hospital trustees but were actually recommended by the appropriations committee. They were constructed directly behind the Administration Building; unfortunately, no photographs of them are known to exist. The Male Convalescent Building, seen in this image, was completed in 1905 with room for 88 patients.

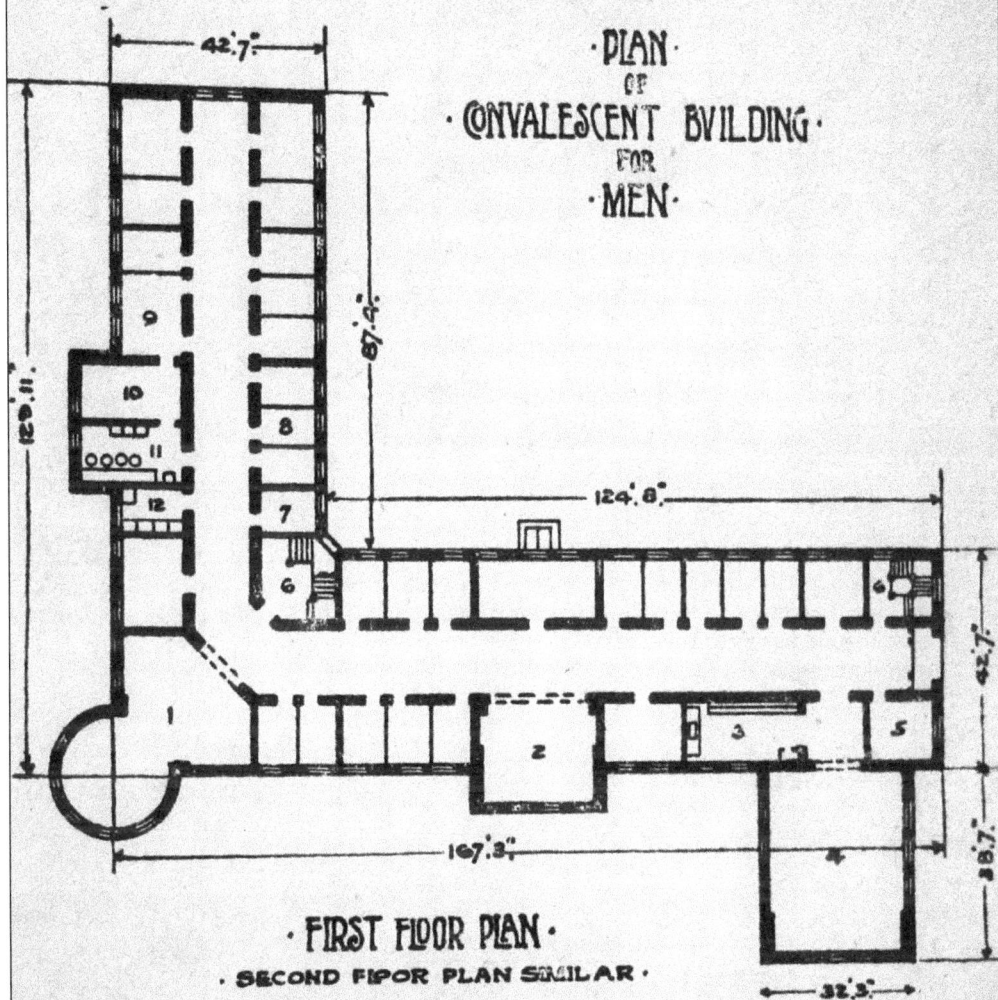

· PLAN ·
OF
· CONVALESCENT BVILDING ·
FOR
· MEN ·

42'.7"

87'.4"

124'.8"

42'.7"

28'.7"

32'.3"

167'.3"

· FIRST FLOOR PLAN ·
· SECOND FLOOR PLAN SIMILAR ·

· INDEX ·

1	BILLIARD ROOM.	7	SHOE ROOM.
2	READING ROOM.	8	LINEN ROOM.
3	SERVING PANTRY.	9	CLOTHES ROOM.
4	DINING ROOM.	10	RAIN BATH.
5	RECEPTION ROOM.	11	TOILET.
6	STAIRS.	12	WASH ROOM.

This floor plan for the Male Convalescent Building shows that it consisted mainly of single and double patient rooms. Each room had its own ventilation and heating ducts. Other rooms were designated for billiards, reading, reception, and dining. The second floor mimicked the first. A "rain bath" was located on both floors.

The Male Psychopathic Building was completed in 1906. It mimicked many of the features of the Male Convalescent Building. To help protect against fire, the floors and partitions in the psychopathic buildings were made of terra-cotta. The stairs were constructed of iron posts and risers, with slate treads.

Both the Male and Female Psychopathic Buildings would later be used for new admissions to the hospital until 1951, when a new Admissions Building was completed.

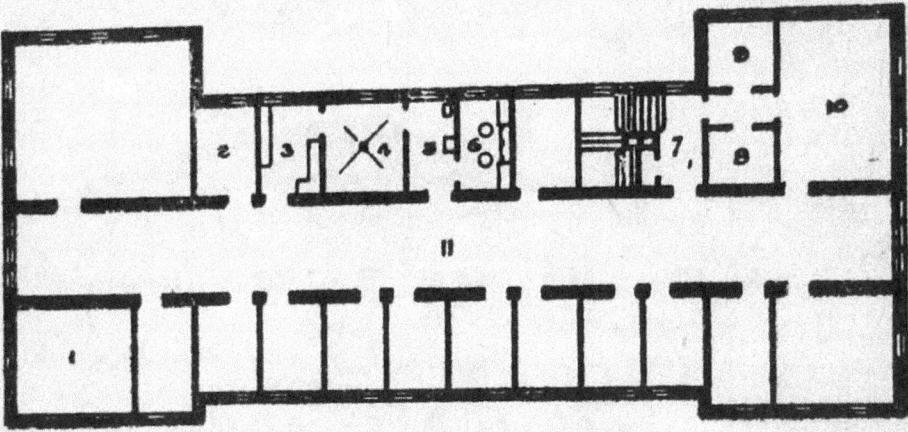

· SECOND FLOOR PLAN ·

· INDEX ·

1 DAY ROOM.	8 DARK ROOM.
2 LINEN ROOM.	9 SURGEONS ROOM
3 CLOTHES ROOM	10 OPERATING ROOM.
4 BATH ROOM.	11 CORRIDOR.
5 WASH ROOM.	12 DINING ROOM.
6 TOILET.	13 PANTRY.
7 STAIRS.	14 RECEPTION ROOM.

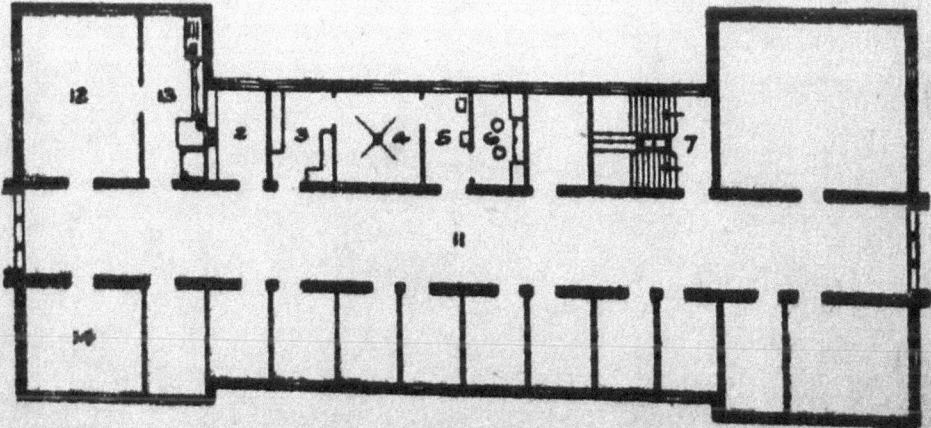

· FIRST FLOOR PLAN ·

The floor plan for the Male Psychopathic Building shows a pretty simple design. The building consisted of two stories with a single double-loaded corridor running down the middle.

49

The Male Dangerous and Destructive Building was also completed in 1906. This structure was one of the largest of the new patient buildings. Unlike the Convalescent and Psychopathic Buildings, this one and its female counterpart consisted mainly of single-loaded corridors; that is, patient rooms lined only one side of the hallway.

Annexes would later be built onto both the male and female buildings, but for the most part, they still retain the same appearance today as they did the day they were completed.

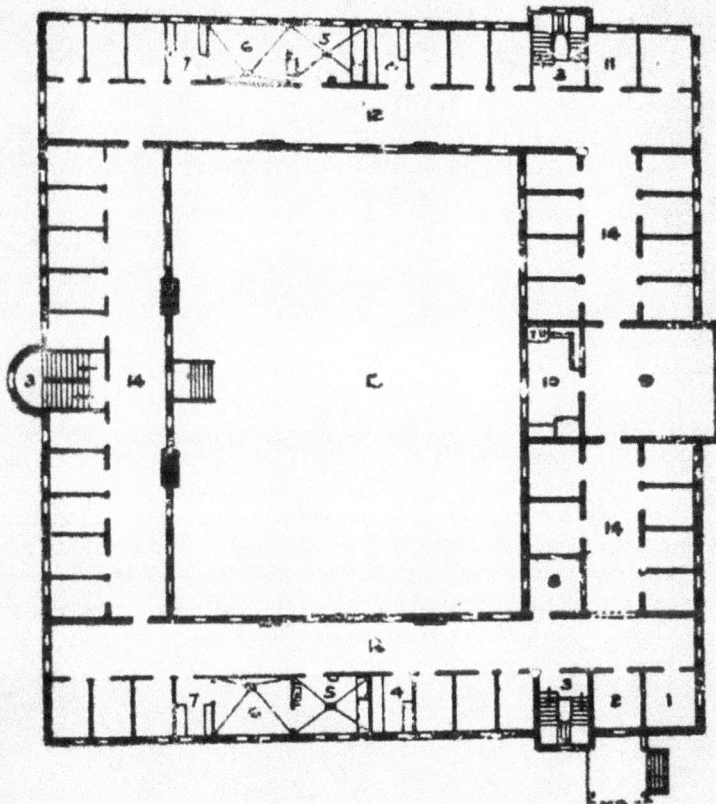

·FIRST FLOOR PLAN·
OF
·DANGEROUS AND DESTRUCTIVE BUILDING·
FOR
·MEN·

·INDEX·

1 VISITORS ROOM
2 MAIN ENTRANCE
3 STAIRS
4 LINEN ROOM
5 TOILET
6 BATH ROOM
7 CLOTHES ROOM

8 SHOE ROOM.
9 DINING ROOM.
10 SERVING ROOM.
11 ATTENDENTS ROOM
12 CORRIDOR DAY ROOM
13 LIGHT WELL
14 CORRIDOR

This floor plan of the Male Dangerous and Destructive Building shows many of its unique features, the most noticeable of which is the large open-air courtyard in the center. Due to the type of patients who lived in this building, it wasn't favorable to allow them open access to the hospital grounds. Rather than construct an unsightly fence around the entire structure, it was purposely designed with an area in the center to be used for outdoor recreation.

In 1905, appropriations were made for the Female Nurses Home. The building was a great relief to the hospital staff that had previously been sleeping in crowded rooms and sometimes even in the patient wards. Construction began on the building in 1906. Constructed in a ravine, it required 10,000 cubic yards of ground fill in order to complete the foundation; to save money, this work was done exclusively by patients. Due to increasing construction costs and state budget cuts, the Female Nurses Home was constructed mostly of wood. Constructing a building of non-fireproof materials was not a popular choice in the eyes of the hospital trustees, but so dire was their need for the new nurses' home that they moved forward and constructed the best building possible with the funds available. A third floor was added later, in 1922.

·FLOOR PLANS·
OF
·NVRSES HOME·

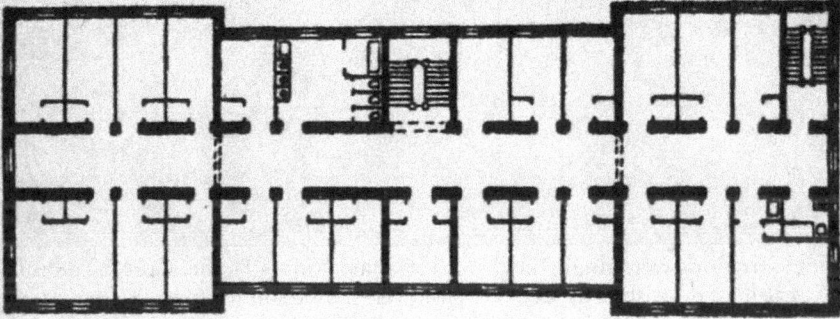

·SECOND FLOOR PLAN·

·THIRD FLOOR PLAN SIMILAR·

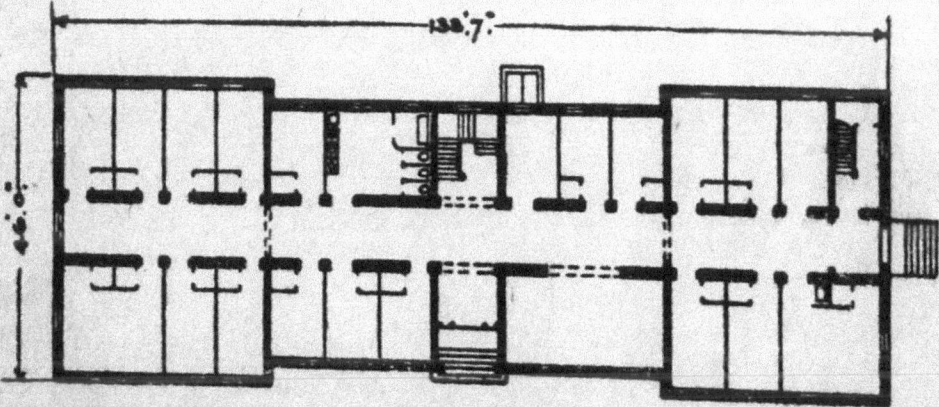

·FIRST·FLOOR·PLAN·

The floor plan for the Female Nurses Home shows its simple design, containing a single bathroom on each floor and single and double bedrooms on either side of the hallway. The Male Nurses Home was built identical to this plan.

In 1909, appropriations were finally made for the Male Nurses Home. Construction began in the spring of 1910 and finished up in 1913. However, the building would sit empty for another year until additional funds became available to furnish it. It was constructed in the same non-fireproof manner as the female home. Fireproof stairwells were added on the side of both nurses' homes a few years later.

ONE OF THE BUILDINGS OF THE PENNA. STATE LUNATIC HOSPITAL, HARRISBURG, PA.
7983 Feet of Indirect Radiation.
Installed by JOHN G. SCHAUM, 107-109 South Water St., Lancaster, Pa.

This postcard shows the newly finished Female Dangerous and Destructive Building. The female building was almost identical to its male counterpart, with the exception of being slightly narrower, most likely due to the ravine that ran along the side of the property. With the completion of this new building in 1907, plans were made to demolish additional sections of the old Main Building. (Author's collection.)

54

The building for psychopathic female patients was finally ready for occupancy on October 1, 1907. It and the Female Convalescent Building were actually completed on July 31 of the same year but were delayed in being turned over to the hospital trustees.

This unreleased postcard shows the Female Convalescent Building shortly after its completion. The vacant land in the foreground is where the female wing of the Main Building stood only a short time earlier.

Appropriations for a new chapel were finally granted in 1911, though only $35,000 was made available out of the original $55,000 that the hospital trustees had requested from the state. Despite this setback, plans moved forward, and the building was completed in 1913. The chapel would sit empty for another year until funds were available to furnish it. It finally opened on February 15, 1914.

Religious services were held in the new 450-seat chapel every Sunday, and prayer meetings were held four times a week. The Catholic Church conducted services every fourth Sunday. It was also used for movies, parties, and special events. (Courtesy of the Pennsylvania Department of Public Welfare.)

Work began on the Sun Parlor in 1910, but there were many construction delays, and it was not completed until 1914 or 1915.

The Sun Parlor was one of the most unique buildings at the hospital and quite possibly in all of the Pennsylvania state hospital system at that time. It featured a very distinctive iron and glass dome topped off with a copper belvedere. The building consisted of just a main floor and basement. Unfortunately, it was soon discovered that the building's most unique feature was also its most costly in terms of heating and maintenance.

This sketch of the interior of the Sun Parlor is the only image of the inside of the building that currently exists in archive collections. It shows the main floor and iron and glass dome. The dome was lined with 40 electric lights around the outer ring, while a cluster of 10 lights hung from the center. Large comfortable sofas and palm trees adorn the floor space, while what looks like a small bar sits to the rear. The main floor also contained a pharmacy and medicine store room. The Sun Parlor was one of the few buildings at the hospital in which men and women were allowed to congregate together; it was also one of the few that had both men's and women's toilets. Weekly dance classes and calisthenics were held under the glass dome, as well as the annual Masked Ball. The basement was divided up into several sections that were used as work areas.

This aerial photograph, taken around 1915, shows the result of 20 years of reconstruction. While all the buildings were now complete, it is obvious that much grading work still needed to be done on the grounds.

Taken before 1927, this image shows in great detail the layout of the new buildings. This building style was referred to as the Cottage Plan. The idea was to have separate buildings for each classification of patient. The buildings were to be no more than two stories in height and should have more of a "home" feeling as opposed to the large single-building institutions of the 1800s. (Courtesy of the Pennsylvania Department of Public Welfare.)

These two photographs show the original entrance to the hospital. Built in 1915, the gate was designed by J.G. Basinger of New York. A gate house was also constructed, the front of which can be seen behind the fence on the left.

Later, as the city grew up around the hospital, the gate was torn down when the new intersection of Cameron Street and Arsenal Boulevard was built. The hospital entrance was moved farther down Cameron Street to its current location across from the State Farm Show Complex. (Courtesy of the Harrisburg State Hospital Historical Society.)

Four

SUPPORTING A CITY

For the hospital to be successful it was essential that it be as self-supporting as possible. A boiler house to provide heat and power equipment, a waterworks to supply fresh water, and a farm to grow crops and raise livestock were all established by 1856. All this, of course, was useless without the manpower to go along with it. Patient labor was also critical to the success of the hospital. Able patients would work on the farm, planting and harvesting crops or tending the animals. They would plant flowers, mow grass, shovel snow, and even help construct buildings. All this was intended to help the patients, to give them a sense of pride and purpose, and to prevent them from just sitting idle in a day room. Attendants and staff would instruct and supervise the work being done. This labor was also useful in helping patients leave the hospital, as it would familiarize them with and train them on skills needed outside the hospital.

The very first boiler house, seen here around 1900, was located in the cellar of the bake house. The boilers generated steam to heat the hospital as well as run some steam-driven equipment. Heating provisions for the original hospital buildings were awarded to Birkinbine and Trotter out of Philadelphia. Their contract for $12,200 was for the construction of the laundry as well as the installation of heating apparatus and steam pipes. They installed two 40-foot-long boilers; steam produced by the boilers was piped to the Main Building through eight-inch cast-iron pipes. In the dirt cellar under the Main Building were "steam coils," which were essentially radiators that heated the air as it traveled though the cellar. The heated air would then rise up into the building via a system of flues. The total system contained 16,000 feet of pipe.

As the hospital grew, a new boiler house was constructed in 1887 at a cost of $45,000. It was used until the 1930s, when a third building for the same purpose was constructed to replace it. One of the most noticeable features of this building was the five-story tower that contained water tanks for the laundry.

This 1930s photograph shows the rear of the new Boiler House. This building housed not only the steam boilers that heated the hospital but also the laundry operations and staff living quarters.

· FLOOR PLANS ·
OF
· BOILER HOUSE ·

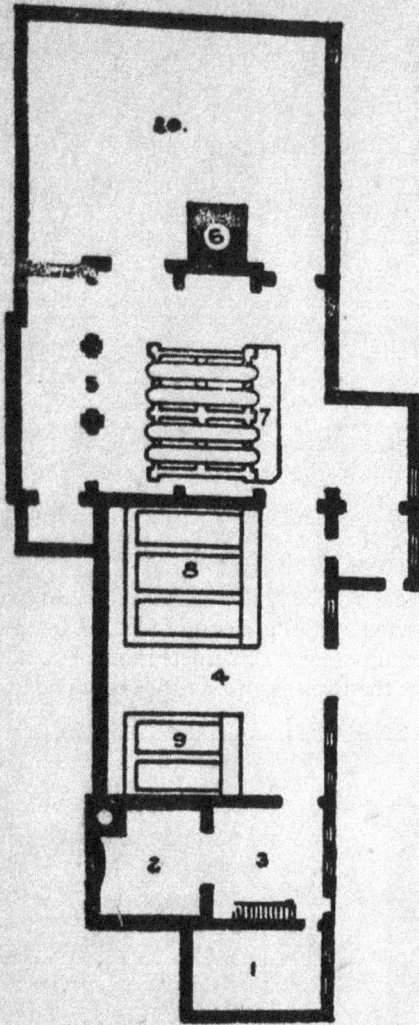

· BOILER FLOOR ·

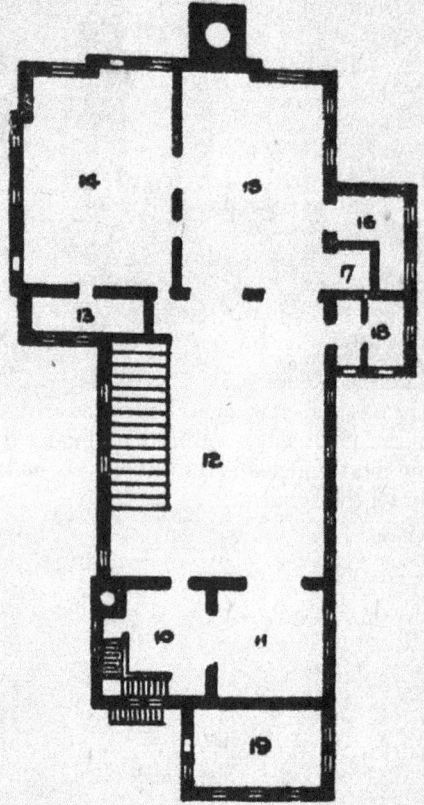

· LAYNDRY FLOOR ·

· INDEX ·

1	DYNAMO ROOM	10	TOWER
2	TANK ROOM.	11	ASSORTING ROOM
3	PVMP ROOM	12	DRYING ROOM.
4	BOILER ROOM.	13	SOAP ROOM.
5	COAL ROOM	14	WASH ROOM.
6	STACK	15	IRONING ROOM
7	BOILERS 600 H.P.	16	STARCHING ROOM
8	BOILERS 450 H.P.	17	STOVE ROOM.
9	BOILERS 160 H.P.	18	TOILET.
20	COAL STORAGE	19	MACHINE SHOP.

The floor plan of the Boiler House shows both the basement, where the boilers were, and the first floor, which was used for the laundry.

The basement contained several sets of boilers, which when combined totaled 1,210 horsepower. They were fired by coal, which was shoveled by hand. The steam created by the boilers was used to run machinery as well as to heat all the hospital buildings.

This undated photograph shows a worker removing ash from the boilers. Coal was transported to the hospital from a wharf on the Susquehanna River by horse and wagon.

In 1893, a 250-kilowatt electric light plant was installed at a cost of $10,000. This undated photograph was taken in the dynamo room of the boiler house. The two large engines seen here were powered by steam from the boilers. Belts turned the dynamos at a high rate of speed, generating the electricity.

This photograph was also taken in the dynamo room but from the opposite side from the image above. It shows two men standing at the control panel behind the dynamos. The electricity passed through a series of breakers before being sent to the hospital buildings to power electric lights and other devices.

This undated photograph shows additional controls and breakers for the electric plant. It was taken at a time when electricity was in its infancy, as evident by the exposed fuses on the left of the panel. Before the electric light plant was installed, the hospital was lighted by gas provided by the Harrisburg Gas Company.

This undated image, taken in the engine room of the Boiler House, shows engineer Davey D. sitting next to a pair of engines. According to the caption, the engines are a "Two Compound" and a "Westinghouse Turbine."

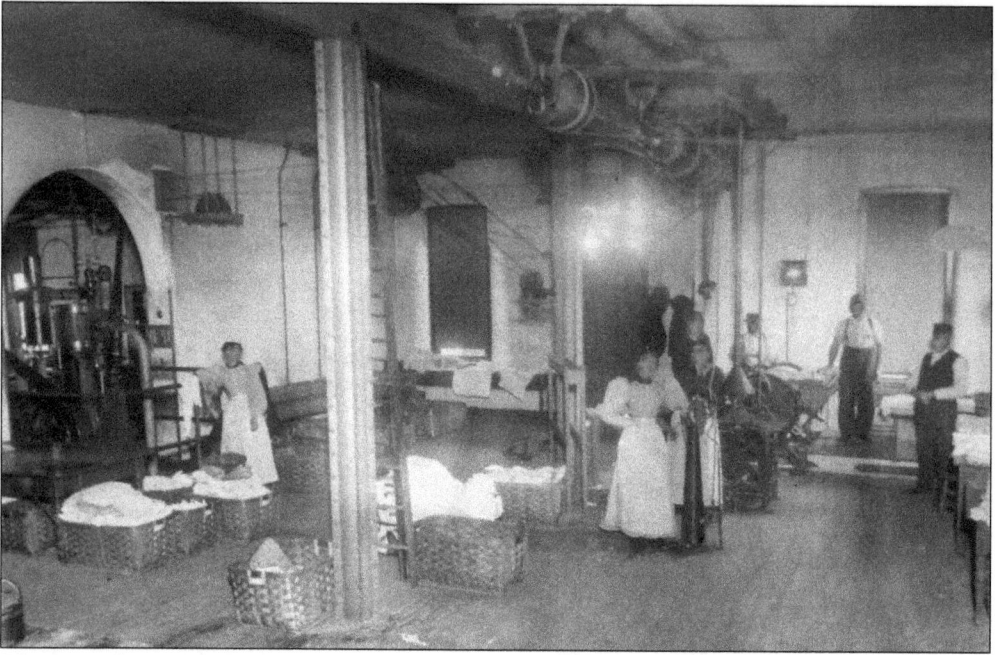

The main floor of the Boiler House contained all the hospital's laundry operations.

This undated photograph shows several women working in the garment repair shop. Most of the clothes that patients wore, as well as their bedding, were all made at the hospital.

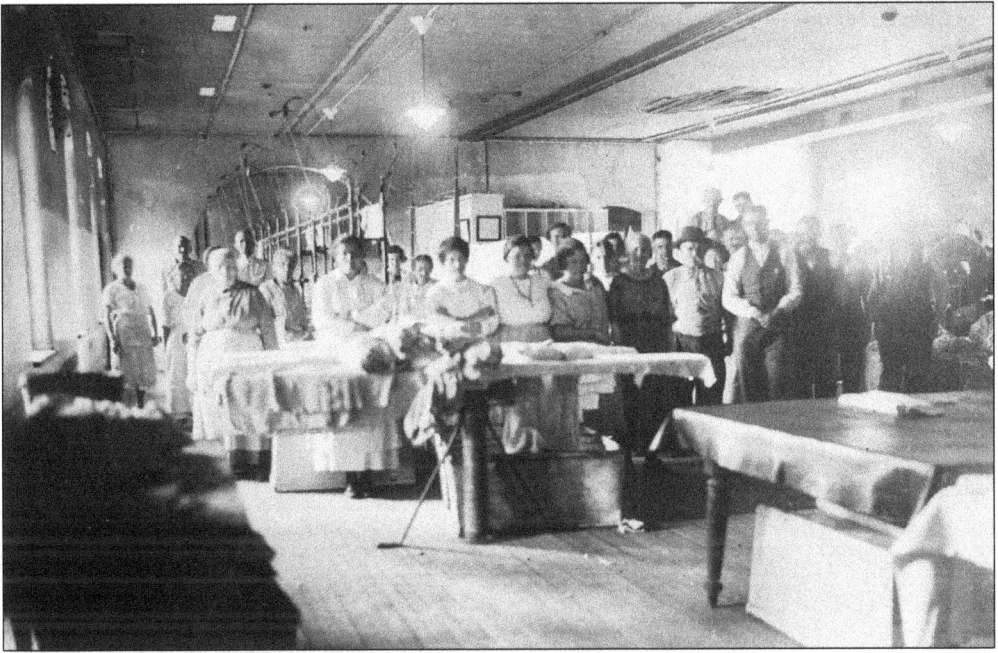

Laundry workers pose for this undated photograph. The majority of work in the laundry during the early years of the hospital was done by female patients.

This image shows men working in the laundry around 1930.

This 1945 photograph shows male patients moving bags of laundry by wagon.

The Boiler House also contained a machine shop on the main floor. This undated photograph shows a workman standing behind some of the belt-driven machinery. This same equipment still remains in the building as of 2012.

The waterworks was established in 1856. It was located in a valley to the south of the main hospital complex. This series of structures handled all the water and sewage processing for the hospital. For much of the early years, the hospital operated completely independent from city services. (Courtesy of William R.)

A dam capable of holding about 400,000 gallons of water was built; it was supplied by a stream that crossed the property. The water was driven through a sand filter bed, and a steam engine pumped it up the hill to tanks in the laundry tower and the Main Building. This image shows an overview of the early waterworks around 1900.

Early sources of water included a stream that crossed the property and an artesian well. Despite having multiple sources of water as well as a reservoir capable of holding a one-week supply, water shortages plagued the hospital for much of its early years. In 1895, a connection was made to the city water supply that could be called upon in an emergency.

The Pump House, seen in this undated photograph, contained steam-powered pumps that sent the water from the valley up the hill to the main complex.

In 1897, work began on two large filter beds. When completed in 1899, it was reported that 98 percent of bacteria was now being removed from the water supply. Daily tests were conducted by the hospital pathologist on both the fresh water supply and the sewage. Results of the tests were tracked and published in annual reports.

This photograph shows two men standing by one of the newly completed filter beds.

Ice Ponds and Pump House

This unreleased postcard shows an aerial view of the newly expanded waterworks, with the two new filter beds in the center. To the left is the Pump House, and to the far rear is the Ice House and pond.

Constructed in 1887, the Ice House provided a storage place for the large blocks of ice harvested from the pond during the winter months. The building was so well insulated that ice could last anywhere from one to two years. This scenic photograph of the Ice House and pond was taken during the first snow of the season on October 30, 1925.

This undated image shows part of the Ice House with the hospital farm in the distance.

This photograph, taken on January 3, 1927, shows several children skating on the frozen pond.

At 10:30 p.m. on March 8, 1927, the Ice House was destroyed by a fire that was set by a patient. It burned to the ground before anything could be done to stop it, its straw insulation and wooden walls leaving little hope of saving the structure. The practice of harvesting and storing ice was actually discontinued several years prior to the fire, when in 1904 the new Cold Storage Building was completed. The remains of the building were removed and the foundation filled in.

This undated image shows a small section of the Ice House and the pond.

After the fire, the pond was eventually filled in and trees were planted. Today this area is part of a nature trail used for hiking and bicycling; the average person would probably never even know that a pond once existed here.

The first farm was put under hospital control in April 1851. It was 130 acres in size, though only 60 acres were usable because much of it was either on steep hillsides or under water. The farm in general needed much work because of the neglected condition it was left in by the previous owner.

Despite the condition of the farm, the yield from the first year was rather good. In the first week of June, 1,100 bushels of potatoes were harvested; the potatoes were considered such good quality that they won an award at the State Agricultural Fair in Lancaster.

In late May, a garden was laid out directly behind the Main Building. The garden supplied such an abundance of vegetables that there was actually a surplus, which was sold at a market in Harrisburg. All work at the farm and in the garden was done by patients under the supervision of attendants and staff.

A greenhouse was constructed later to supply the hospital with a year-round supply of plants and seeds. The farm produced a wide variety of vegetables and fruits such as squash, onions, lettuce, cucumbers, carrots, beans, cabbage, tomatoes, kale, mushrooms, grapes, and raspberries. There was a separate garden for herbs that provided many of the spices the kitchen used.

In 1938, the hospital owned about 400 tillable acres. Dairy cattle furnished a large part of the milk consumed by patients and staff. The piggery provided 35,000 pounds of pork annually, and the pigs consumed much of the garbage from the hospital. By 1963, the hospital consumed in one day 100 pounds of coffee, 300 dozen eggs, 1,200 pounds of meat, 1,200 to 1,500 loaves of bread, 550 pies (when served), 1,000 pounds of potatoes, 35 bushels of fresh vegetables, and 120 gallons of canned fruits or vegetables. Eighty percent of the vegetables consumed were grown on the farm, totaling about one million pounds' worth. Over one pint of milk per person was produced by the dairy herd. Because of this self-sustaining ability, the average cost of care per patient was kept low at $4.40 a day. (Courtesy of the Harrisburg State Hospital Historical Society.)

"Chore horses" were used on the farm to plow the fields. When the horses were not working at the hospital they were often hired to haul coal from the wharf to neighboring businesses. The building in the background was most likely the horse stable.

Workers tear down the old dairy barn in this undated photograph. The barn was located at the front of the hospital property and was considered for many years to be too close to the city. Complaints about the smell from the barn and the piggery, which was also located at the front of the property, were received often from townspeople who lived close to the hospital.

Appropriations for a new dairy barn were granted in 1917, but the amount was too small to construct a barn big enough for the hospital's needs. Additional appropriations were granted in 1930, and construction commenced on the new barn.

The annual report from the year the new dairy barn was completed is unfortunately unavailable, so no data exists on the physical size and capacity of the barn. But it is obvious from photographs that the new barn was significantly larger than the one it replaced, and its placement at the rear of the hospital property kept it away from the ever-growing city of Harrisburg.

Five

THE PEAK OF STATE CARE

It didn't take long after the final new buildings opened in 1914 for overcrowding problems to return. By 1921, there were 1,319 patients in buildings designed to hold only 1,000. Much of this overcrowding was due to an increasing number of patients with no true mental illness. Homeless, elderly, alcoholics, drug addicts, and those who were generally seen as unfavorable elements in their communities were all being sent to the hospital. This problem was not isolated to Harrisburg; state hospitals all over the country saw their populations balloon through the 1950s. Harrisburg, however, took a different approach to this problem than other state hospitals. Rather than constructing lots of big and expensive-to-maintain buildings, the hospital used a parole system and outpatient clinics to combat much of the overcrowding. In the 1930s, there were weekly parole meetings where staff members would interview potential parolees; later, that frequency increased to two times a week. The overcrowded conditions of the hospital were not only difficult on the patients, some of whom were once again sleeping in hallways, they were also a strain on hospital resources. Critical services like the kitchen, laundry, and power plant were running well over capacity to keep up with the increasing population. Despite extensive use of the parole system, it was inevitable that the hospital would eventually need to expand. The campus would undergo two major expansion periods, first in the 1930s, which was focused mainly on expanding existing buildings, and then again in the 1950s, when three new patient buildings were constructed.

Around 1930, construction began on a second floor for the Infirmary. The building, which was previously constructed mostly of wood, was updated and modernized. Narrow stairwells in the center section were replaced, and the building was made much more fireproof.

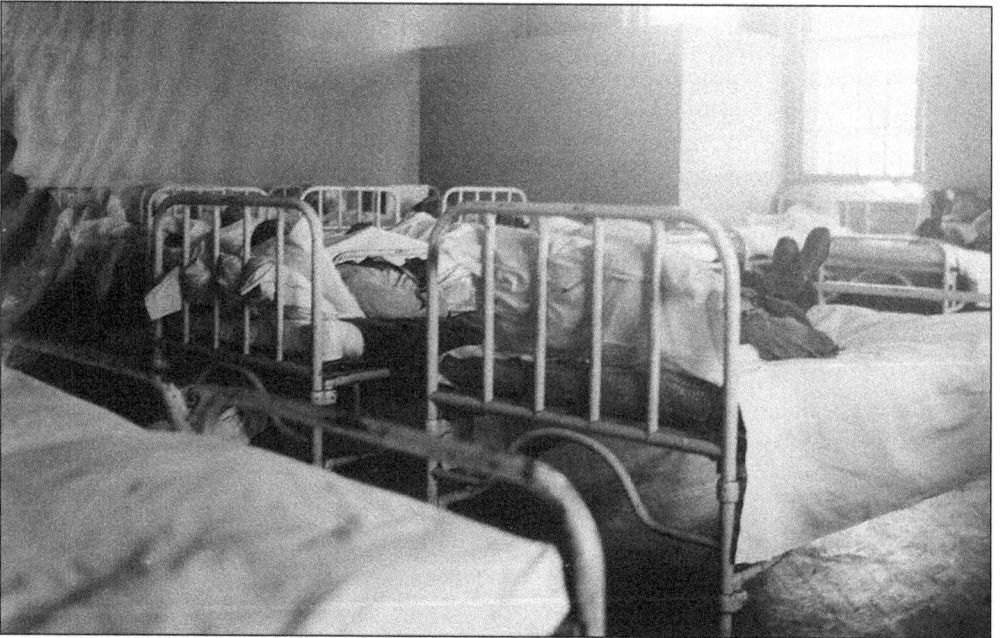

This dormitory on the second floor of the Infirmary housed tuberculosis patients until a dedicated building was completed in 1938. The conditions were crowded, and the Infirmary building lacked any of the features needed in a proper tuberculosis hospital of the period.

Taken around 1933, this aerial photograph shows some early expansion of the patient buildings. Annexes have been built onto both buildings for dangerous and destructive patients, as well as an addition to the rear of both Branch Buildings. At the rear of the campus, a new two-story building for married employees has been completed, and a third floor has also been added to the Female Nurses Home.

In 1933, construction started on a new building that would become the Hospital for the Physically Ill. It was much like a general hospital, housing a surgical suite, x-ray lab, dentist office, pharmacy, occupational therapy shops, and classrooms. The main section of the building was comprised of two floors and contained mostly single- and double-patient rooms. The wings contained large dormitories.

This photograph, taken from the top of the Laundry Tower around 1935, shows much of the hospital campus. In the center is the completed Hospital for the Physically Ill. In the foreground is the roof of the South Branch Building and to the right are the Infirmary and the Male Nurses Home. (Courtesy of William R.)

A new building for patients with tuberculosis was completed in 1938. The construction of a dedicated tuberculosis building was put off for several years in favor of moving infected patients to a dedicated hospital elsewhere in the state. The finished building was two stories tall; it had large open day rooms on either end and was capable of holding 140 patients. (Author's collection.)

By the 1930s, the Sun Parlor was seen as a rather useless building. It required much more money to maintain than other buildings due to the glass dome. It was decided to replace the dome and divide the building up into three stories, the first and second floors being for offices and the third for staff living quarters. Once renovations were completed, it became known as the Medical Center.

In 1938, a new power plant was constructed in the valley behind the Female Nurses Home. Once completed, all the steam boilers and power generating equipment were removed from the old Boiler House and the laundry operations were expanded throughout the entire building. (Author's collection)

This undated photograph shows the open space between the original kitchen (right) and the North Branch Building (left) where a new kitchen addition would be built.

The new Central Kitchen was finished in 1937; it included a much larger food preparation area, numerous walk-in freezers, and a large dining area with a seating capacity of 700 patients. A modern dock allowed for easy unloading of larger trucks, and the basement contained several storage rooms. The Central Kitchen served about four and a half tons of food daily in the 1950s. (Author's collection.)

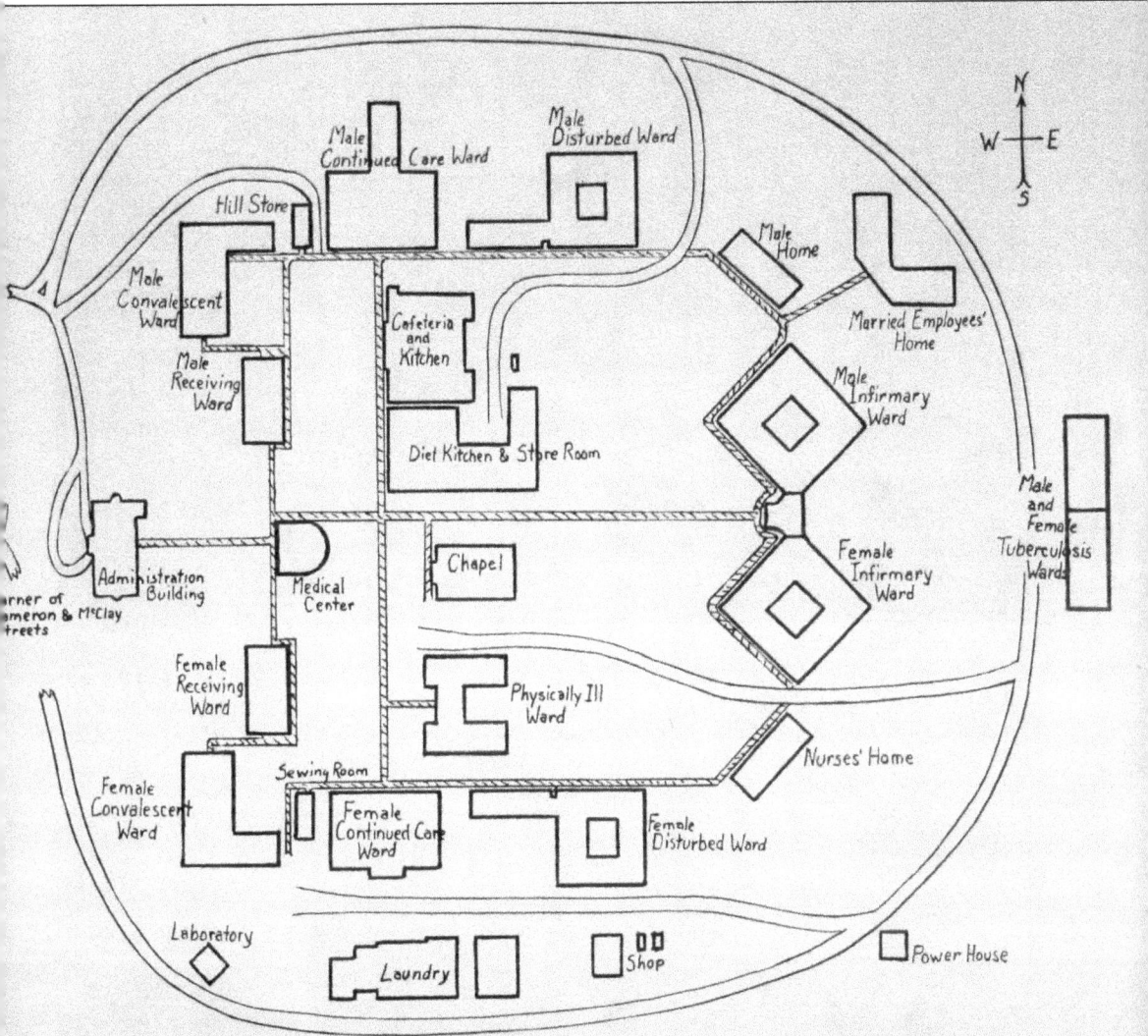

Male Continued Care Ward

Male Disturbed Ward

Hill Store

Male Home

Male Convalescent Ward

Cafeteria and Kitchen

Married Employees' Home

Male Receiving Ward

Male Infirmary Ward

Diet Kitchen & Store Room

Male and Female Tuberculosis Wards

Administration Building

Medical Center

Chapel

Female Infirmary Ward

corner of Cameron & McClay Streets

Female Receiving Ward

Physically Ill Ward

Female Convalescent Ward

Sewing Room

Nurses' Home

Female Continued Care Ward

Female Disturbed Ward

Laboratory

Laundry

Shop

Power House

N
W — E
S

This map of the hospital was likely created around 1940. It shows all the original buildings as well as several new ones that were built in the 1930s. It also shows the tunnel system that linked all the buildings together. The tunnels were used to move from building to building during the winter months. They also carried utilities, such as water and steam, to all the buildings. With the 1930s expansion now completed, the patient capacity of the hospital increased to about 2,000. But by 1948, the population again well exceeded capacity, with 2,472 in house and 511 additional patients on parole. The new goal of the superintendent and trustees in the 1950s was to bring the hospital capacity up to 3,000. (Courtesy of the Pennsylvania Department of Public Welfare.)

This unreleased postcard shows an aerial view of the hospital around 1950. In the upper right is the newly completed Tuberculosis Building. Next to it is a large area of land that has been recently cleared of grass and trees; this is where construction is commencing on the new building for acutely disturbed women. In the center left is another recently cleared plot of land where the new Admissions Building is being constructed. (Author's collection.)

By the 1950s, both Branch Buildings had been in use for much longer than anyone probably could have predicted when they were constructed. Hastily built, they were constructed primarily of wood and were considered fire hazards. The hospital superintendent and trustees wanted to either renovate or replace them in the 1930s, but no appropriations were made by the state.

This photograph shows the new building for acute female patients at upper left. Based on the appearance of the landscape around the building, this photograph was probably taken around 1951 or 1952, just as the building was being completed. In the center is the smoke stack of the new Boiler House, which was completed in 1938. (Courtesy of William R.)

A new building for acutely disturbed women was constructed in 1951. Later known as Hillcrest, it was designed to hold 145 patients for long-term care. The building was comprised of mainly open dormitories that allowed for easier supervision of this "overactive" class of patients. (Author's collection.)

In 1951, a new one-million-square-foot Admissions Building was constructed at a cost of $1.25 million. It had wards for both male and female patients, with a total capacity of 200. New admissions were seen as a high priority; it was believed that the sooner treatment began for a newly diagnosed patient, the better his or her chances were for a fast recovery. All new admissions to the hospital would reside in this building for an evaluation period of about 30 to 90 days. If no improvement was seen, they would be moved to an appropriate ward with other patients of the same classification. The new Admissions Building was the largest building at the hospital until the completion of Eaton a few years later. It was three stories tall and was comprised of mostly single-patient rooms. Other features included a library, barbershop, cafeteria, examination rooms, a clinical laboratory, hydrotherapy rooms, two occupational therapy rooms, and a larger nursing staff than most other wards.

This photograph of the rear of the new Admissions Building was taken just as construction had finished. From this angle, it can be seen how the new building was seemingly constructed around what was once known as the Sun Parlor. A hallway was built to connect the two buildings. (Courtesy of William R.)

This aerial image of the front of the campus provides a good view of the new Admissions Building as well as the new Central Kitchen (lower left). Notice how much larger the new buildings are compared to their older counterparts built between 1900 and 1910.

The final building project of the 1950s was the patient building known simply as Eaton. Construction started in early 1958, with a projected completion date around the end of 1959 and the beginning of 1960. When completed, Eaton would be the largest building at the hospital, with a patient capacity of 250. It had its own kitchen, library, dentist office, hair salon, hydrotherapy rooms, and gymnasium. Eaton was originally intended to be the counterpart of the Female Acute Building, housing only male patients of the same classification for long-term care. However, around this same time, the North and South Branch Buildings, which were built in 1886, were condemned as fire hazards and were no longer suitable for housing patients. Once Eaton was completed, both the branch buildings were emptied and demolished with the intention of erecting new structures in their place; however, new replacement buildings were never constructed. Eaton would house both male and female patients, as well as a variety of patient classifications, until the hospital closed. (Courtesy of William R.)

This and the next three undated photographs were likely taken as construction finished up on Eaton and the building was being furnished. This particular image shows one of the nurse stations. There were six of these stations, one on each ward. To the right of the nurse station (just out of the picture) would have been a hallway that led to a dayroom.

Two men, likely hospital trustees, stand at the entrance to the gymnasium, which was located on the lower level of Eaton.

The Eaton kitchen was capable of feeding the entire building, 700 meals daily. This was extremely helpful in relieving the Central Kitchen, which had seemingly always operated over capacity.

This image shows a newly furnished visiting room on either the second or third floor.

The last new building constructed at the hospital was the Work Advancement Center, in 1963. The curtailment in new building projects was not due to lack of want by the hospital trustees and superintendent. In the last available biennial report of 1958, a list of needed buildings included a recreation hall and gymnasium, an expansion or replacement of the current Chapel, a 300-bed medical and surgical building, and a building for additional administrative office space. Much of this planned expansion was likely needed less and less as the patient population began to fall after the 1960s, when more drugs came into use. The hospital was already spending $140,000 annually on drugs in 1958. This aerial image shows the hospital around 1965.

Six

LIFE ON THE HILL

Superintendent Howard Petry was the first to coin the nickname "City on the Hill" in his 1950–1952 biennial report. This nickname was certainly not far from the truth, as the hospital was like living in a small city. It had everything from a general store to a butcher; it even had a print shop and fire department. Patients and staff lived together on the same campus; even the superintendent and his family lived in the Administration Building. Every Christmas, everyone would gather for music and festivities, and patients would receive some form of gift, even it if was just candy and fruit. Throughout the year, there would be picnics on the lawn, horse shows, baseball and softball games, and a yearly Cherry Blossom Festival. Other leisure activities consisted of playing pool, reading in the library, and playing in the hospital band or orchestra. In the early days, patients would take carriage rides and watch magic lantern shows. Trips into Harrisburg for the fair were common, and some patients would receive weekend passes to leave the hospital on their own. Patients at the hospital would experience a mix of activities. Typically, they would follow a routine consisting of rest, meals, free time on the ward or outside, time working in one of the various shops, and of course, time spent receiving treatments for their illness. Treatment methods for patients varied greatly throughout the 155-year history of the hospital. In the early days, the best available treatment methods were simply good food, plenty of fresh air, and keeping the mind occupied through amusements or work. When the original hospital was built, the idea was to use the actual building as a method of treatment. This was common throughout the United States in the mid- and late 19th century. States would often build enormous Kirkbride-design hospitals with lots of elaborate decoration, open and airy wards, and immaculately manicured lawns and gardens. Harrisburg attempted this method of treatment unsuccessfully with the original Main Building.

The caption on this photograph reads, "George K., head gardener and dogs, about 1900." This man was in charge of overseeing the work done on the grounds and around the new buildings constructed between 1893 and 1910. His responsibilities included filling in the ravine, leveling the ground, planting grass and trees, and supervising the vegetable garden.

The caption on this photograph reads, "Superintendent's driving horse around 1900." Horses were essential at the hospital; they were used for everything from plowing the fields to transportation into Harrisburg.

This undated image shows the hospital band. The band was comprised of both patients and staff. (Author's collection.)

Another photograph, taken around the same time as the one above, shows the hospital orchestra. Just like the band, the orchestra was comprised of both patients and staff. (Author's collection.)

This July 1926 photograph taken outside of the Chapel shows the female baseball team.

The caption on this photograph reads, "Baseball club, June 14, 1926." The hospital ball teams were made up of both patients and staff.

The caption on this June 1925 photograph reads "Harrisburg State Hospital, Champions of 1925, State's team."

The caption on this photograph reads, "Practicing for the horse show, 1951."

This photograph shows Field Day at the hospital on July 4, 1930. There are no details on whether this was an annual event or not, but large events like this would have been common at the hospital.

Another photograph from the 1930 Field Day shows the 50-yard nurses' foot race.

This 1970 photograph shows three patients sitting in a day room in one of the Dangerous and Destructive Buildings.

A group of patients relaxes outside the Male Recreation Building. This building was constructed in 1935 and was also known as Hill Store. Located between the North Branch Building and the Male Convalescent Building, it housed a barbershop, general store, and two pool tables. It was constructed mainly of wood and was torn down in 1975. (Courtesy of William R.)

Male patients spend time in the yard behind Eaton.

Female patients can be seen in this undated photograph participating in occupational therapy. The woman standing is labeled as Mrs. Alma F. Some of the items patients made were sold at a market in Harrisburg; the money would be put towards entertainment for the patients.

This undated image shows the Industrial Shop, which was located in the basement of the Chapel. Patients in this shop made items such as chairs and brooms. It was common for able patients to spend time working around the hospital or in an industrial shop. This method of treatment was known as occupational therapy; it was intended give patients a sense of pride and purpose. By the 1960s, the hospital had established shops for making beds and mattresses, upholstering furniture, printing, sewing, shoe repair, and toys. Men would also work on the farm, mow the lawn, shovel snow, and at times even assist with the construction of buildings. Women would work in the laundry creating and repairing clothing and other fabrics, in the kitchen, and also doing general cleaning tasks around the hospital. This practice ended in 1973 when a law was passed that required working patients to be paid a minimum wage. (Courtesy of the Pennsylvania Department of Public Welfare.)

By 1963, there were approximately 550 patients participating in 14 occupational therapy units. There were also a number of special clubs that patients could join, including a nature club, flower arranging club, hobbies club, and bird watchers club. A patient works a printing press in this undated photograph.

A new Work Advancement Center was completed in 1963. This building was used to teach patients job skills and prepare them for life outside the hospital. This patient appears to be working on drawers for a dresser in the carpentry shop.

This image shows a patient in the Community Living Opportunity Program. In this program, patients would learn how to live on their own by practicing household tasks in a home on the hospital campus.

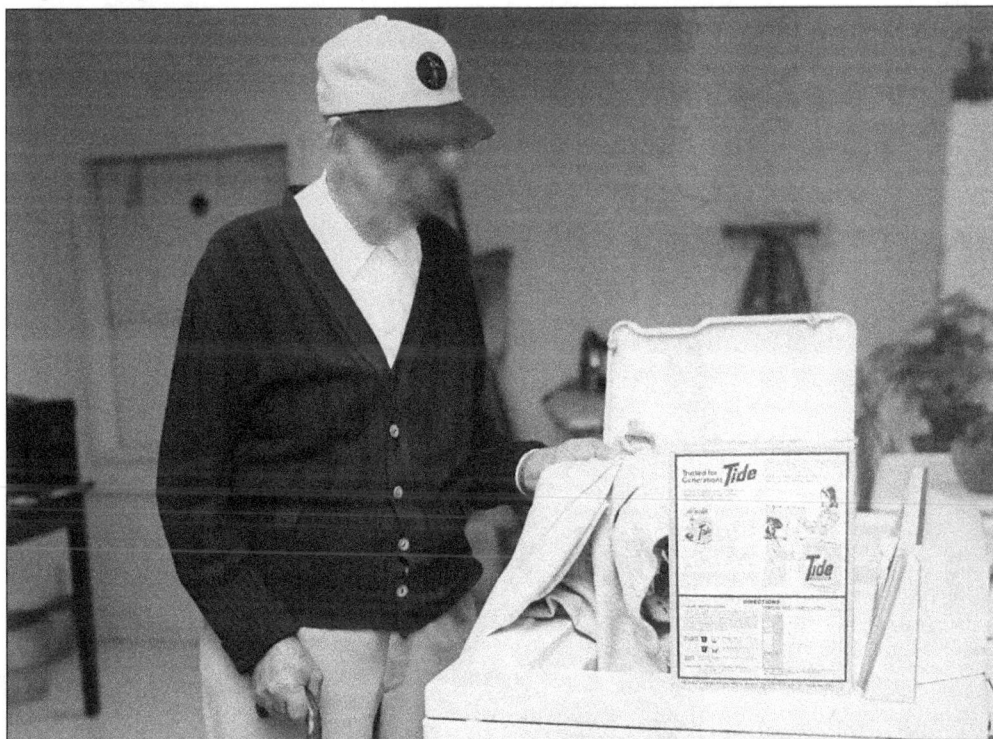

The gentleman in this undated photograph is also in the Community Living Opportunity Program. He is learning how to operate a modern laundry machine in a home setting.

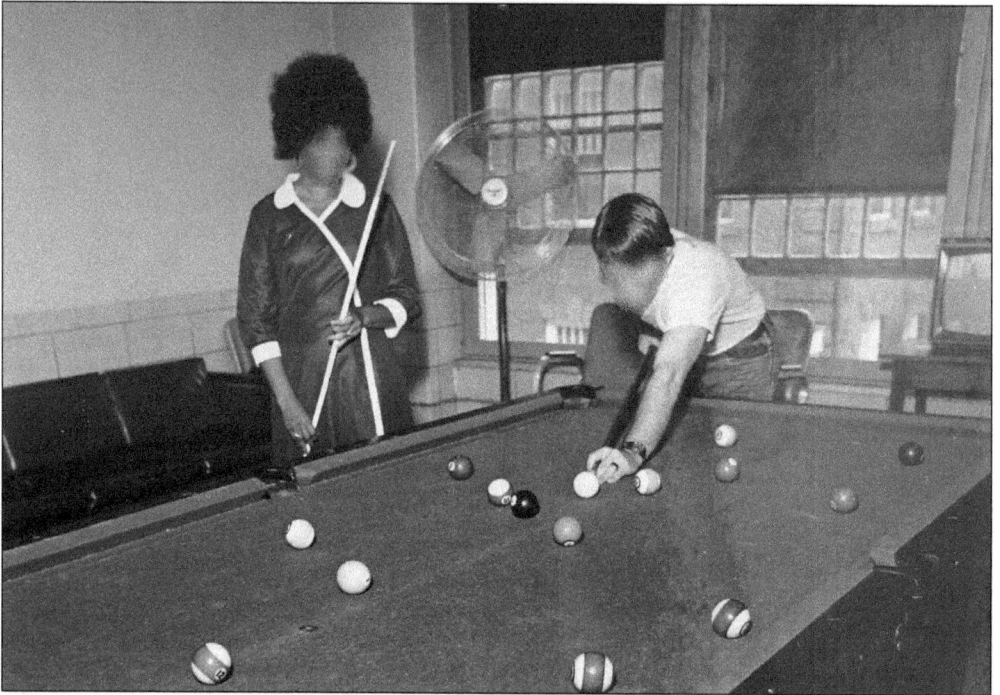

This 1976 photograph shows two patients playing pool. This is one of several images that appear to have been staged by the hospital, possibly for use in a publication.

This photograph shows the same male patient as above. On the back it is labeled as "Psychiatric Treatment Center Cafeteria."

Superintendent Hamblen Eaton stands by a large bookshelf on which sits an artist's rendering of the building that would bear his name.

The Chapel was extensively decorated for the Christmas season, as can been seen in these two undated photographs. (Author's collection.)

Patients and staff would gather in the Chapel for a special Christmas service with festive music. The patients would also receive some form of gift. In the early days, the gifts would often be fruit or candy; sometimes, organizations and private citizens would donate gifts as well.

Several social workers gathered for this undated photograph.

This caption on this undated image reads "Mr. Clarence P. speaking with Miss Margaret M." It is also indicated that Margaret M. is the chief social worker.

This 1967 photograph shows hospital staff interviewing a patient in one of the outpatient clinics.

This November 1962 photograph was taken at one of the annual Old Timer Dinners, a tradition that was started in 1952. Any hospital employee with over 10 years of service was invited to the dinners.

The caption on this undated photograph reads, "Female night watch, Harrisburg State Hospital." The hospital struggled through much of the late 19th and early 20th centuries to fill empty staff and nursing positions. Several factors contributed to this problem, but the two biggest were a lack of adequate on-campus housing and low wages. The city of Harrisburg was an industrial center during the peak years of the hospital, and there were many better-paying jobs available in the immediate vicinity of the hospital. These jobs would often lure away potential applicants. Both world wars also had a serious impact on the hospital, especially on the male side. During World War II, many male staff were drafted into the military. At one point during the war, there was as little as one nurse for every 166 patients. In June 1945, only 26 of 92 open positions on the male side were filled.

The caption on this photograph reads, "Male 8 Cafeteria, Opened April 11, 1960." Male 8 was another name for ward eight in the Male Dangerous and Destructive Building. (Courtesy of the Harrisburg State Hospital Historical Society.)

The description on this photograph does not indicate what building it was taken in, but most of the patient buildings had dining rooms similar to this one. Once the Central Kitchen was expanded in the 1930s, many of these ward dining rooms were converted to dormitories.

Patients would have used the tubs in this undated photograph as part of their hydrotherapy treatment. There were many different methods of this treatment used throughout the years. Another common method, called a "rain bath," was where a patient would stand in a shower stall and an attendant would spray them with various types of nozzles. (Courtesy of the Pennsylvania Department of Public Welfare.)

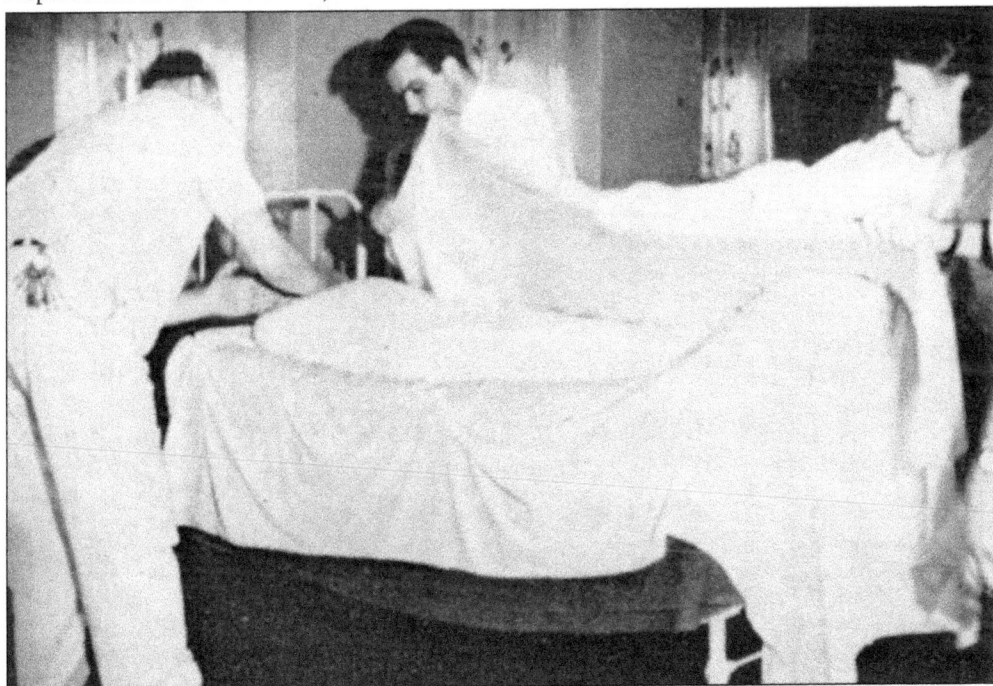

The method of hydrotherapy seen in this photo was called a "wet pack." A patient would lie on a table wrapped in wet sheets for an extended period of time; as the sheets dried, they would shrink and limit the patient's movement. The intention was to calm and restrain an anxious or excited patient. (Courtesy Pennsylvania Department of Public Welfare.)

This photograph, taken around 1940, shows a severely overcrowded dayroom in the South Branch Building. Overcrowding was a fact of life at all state hospitals, including Harrisburg. The crowded conditions at the hospital existed because of the unfortunate way it was used by the outside world.

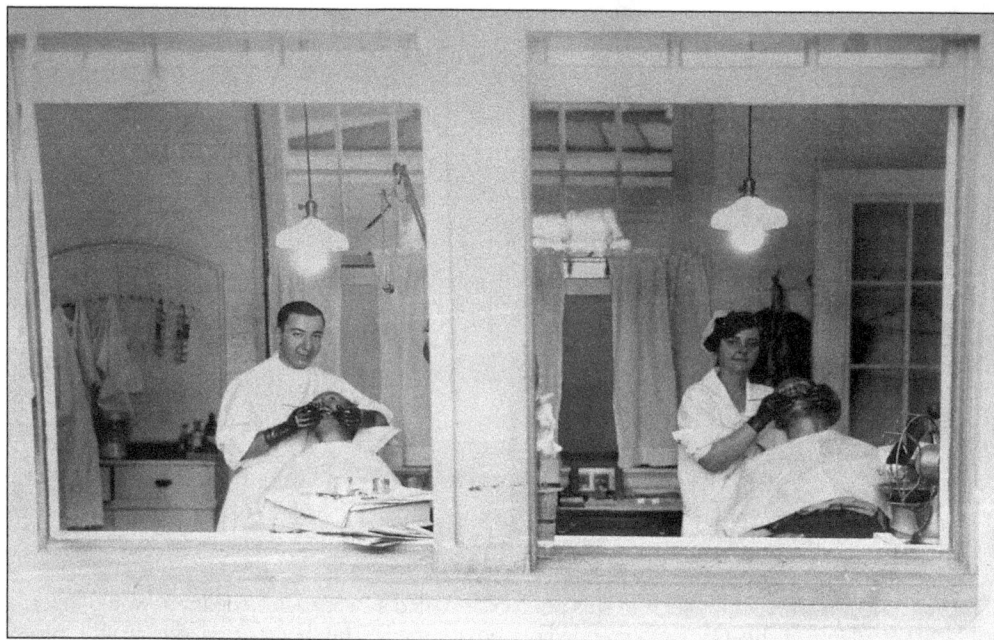

Harrisburg had all the amenities of a small city, including dentist offices in several of the buildings. Two patients receive a check-up in this undated photograph.

Many patients were at the hospital not because of a true mental illness but because they were unwanted in society. Homeless, alcoholics, drug addicts, and even the elderly would be sent to the hospital. (Courtesy of the Pennsylvania Department of Public Welfare.)

In 1954, wards three and four were converted into "open wards." There were no locked doors, and there was only a single nurse per ward. Patients were allowed to come and go as they pleased and spend more time outside.

In 1941, Harrisburg was the first Pennsylvania state hospital to use electroshock therapy on depressed patients. This was before electroshock equipment was available commercially; the hospital constructed its own machine in-house. In 1952, it was again the first hospital in the state to use insulin shock therapy. It was also the first hospital to adopt the malarial treatment of neurosyphilis. Lobotomies were looked upon by the superintendent and trustees with great caution and skepticism. There are many mentions in annual reports of the reluctance to use this method of treatment in-house due to its often adverse side effects. Some patients were lobotomized, but most were sent to Philadelphia or Washington, DC, for the procedure. This undated photograph shows staff meeting with a patient.

Seven

CLOSURE AND NEW LIFE

Throughout the end of the 20th century, the population of the hospital fell rapidly. This was due to a combination of new drugs and a push to return the care of the mentally ill back to community centers and homes. The patient population of Harrisburg State Hospital in 1992 was a mere 450. Only those who had repeated admissions to a county mental health center were being referred to a state hospital. Of those who were still being admitted to the hospital, the average stay was down to six months. The hospital was finally closed on January 27, 2006. Three months prior to the closure, the patient population was down to only 148. It seems that the belief of what is best for the care of those with mental illnesses has come full circle in 200 years. From a push in the 1800s to get people off the streets and into state-run institutions where they could receive 24-hour supervision, in modern times, they are being returned back to the homes and even the streets from which they came. According to the Substance Abuse and Mental Health Care Administration, as of 2009, there were approximately 11 million adults in the United States with a serious mental illness.

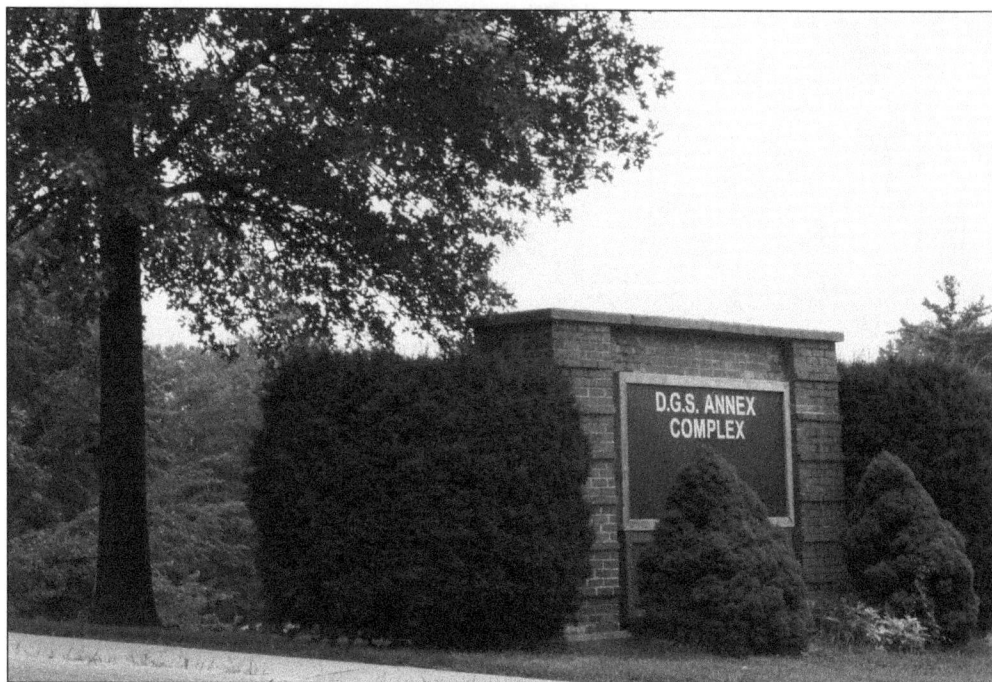

On July 1, 2006, the Pennsylvania Department of General Services assumed responsibility for the former hospital, giving new life to the buildings as office space for state employees. (Author's collection.)

As of 2012, the former hospital buildings still sit atop the hill overlooking the Pennsylvania Farm Show Complex. The campus is a beautiful place to visit on a spring day, with trees lining the many walkways and roads. (Courtesy of William R.)

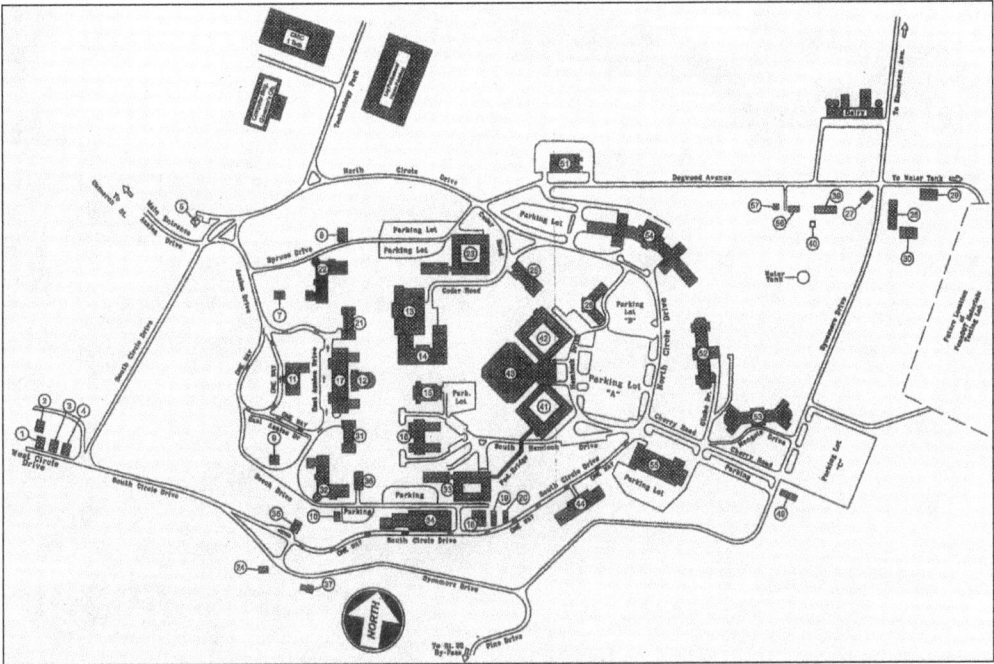

This map shows the former hospital campus as of 2007. With the exception of the Female Nurses Home and both of the Branch Buildings, all the major structures built after 1895 still stand as of 2012. (Author's collection.)

In 1982, this large addition was built onto the front of the Infirmary. The center section of the original building was completely remodeled, and a new entrance was constructed on what was once the rear of the building. Though some effort seemed to have been made to make the addition fit in with the rest of the campus, its architecture still makes it an eyesore among the original buildings. (Author's collection.)

The Canteen was established in the original kitchen building for those who wished to purchase food during hours that the Central Kitchen was not open. All the equipment still sits as if ready to serve patients. (Author's collection.)

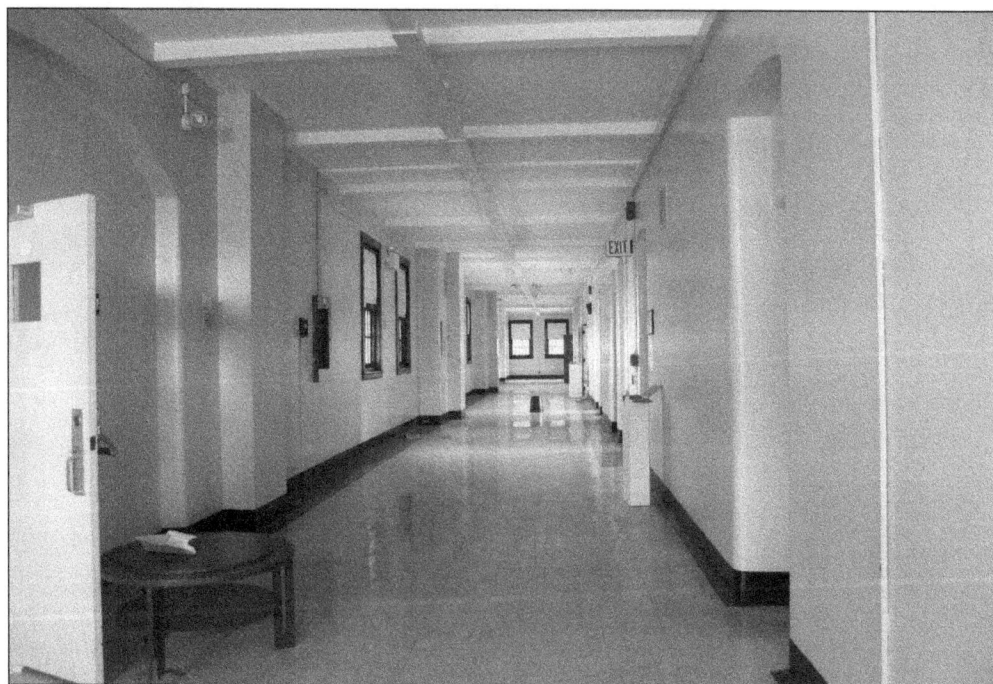

An empty hallway in the Male Dangerous and Destructive Building still looks much as it did when the hospital was in operation. (Author's collection.)

The cornerstone from the Main Building now resides in a brick display next to the Administration Building; however, no one is quite sure how it arrived there. It might have been saved during the demolition in 1895, or it could have been found in 1951 when construction on the Admissions Building foundation unearthed debris from the Main Building. Either way, it is a wonderful reminder of the long history of the hospital. (Author's collection.)

The Administration Building is still in use today as offices for the state. The former superintendent's apartment on the third floor has been painstakingly restored with period furnishings to look like it would have 100 years ago. (Author's collection.)

Visit us at
arcadiapublishing.com